START RIGHT

HOW TO PICK A WINNING BUSINESS IDEA
AND MAKE IT SUCCESSFUL

SANGEETA MULCHANDANI

JUMPSTART STUDIO

JUMPSTART STUDIO

ISBN 9780645911602

Disclaimer

The material in this publication is of the nature of general comment only and does not represent professional advice. It is not intended to provide specific guidance for any particular circumstances, and it should not be relied upon for any decision to take action or not to take action on any matter which it covers. Reader should obtain professional advice where appropriate, before making any such decision. To the maximum extent permitted by law, the author and publisher disclaim all responsibility and liability to any person, arising directly or indirectly from any person taking or not taking action based on the information in this book.

With blessings from Sai Baba,
my eternal guiding light

Contents

Testimonials

"Start Right is a clearly written guide for early-stage entrepreneurs. Sangeeta Mulchandani has condensed many lessons from her years of business experience and her educational journey into a practical and useful handbook. The highlight of the book are the exercises. Each is well developed and if followed, can propel the entrepreneur along the challenging path of finding inspiration, developing problem-solution fit and market entry. The stories are memorable and joyous to read, yet what stands out is the cohesiveness of the book: Sangeeta successfully connects the actual steps an entrepreneur needs to undertake with an overarching framework linking mindset, strategy and execution. The book helps entrepreneurs learn how their hope and passion can be realised through a practical, step-by-step process. Highly recommended."

– Kwanghui Lim, Associate Professor, Melbourne Business School

"Thank you so much, Sangeeta, as a solopreneur this book absolutely opened up my mind and helped to organise my entrepreneurial activities. It is a must-read book and would recommend it to all types of entrepreneurs any day."

– Sheik Nizamuddin, Senior Manager, Information Security

"You have simplified business 101 into your book and even as someone who has some experience behind her, I still learned plenty from your words and guidance. Your book is inspiring, actionable and thought-provoking. It's a handy guide that will support any new business owner to move forward and turn their dream into a reality."

– Natalie Moore, Co-founder, Own Your Health Collective

"This book is better than Google if you are up at night wondering how to take the steps to founding your own business. It will be dog-eared and kept in your back pocket in the most crucial stages of early business development. If you take the lessons on board and do the work, you will be forging a great path for yourself and save yourself the time and heartache of the many mistakes and pitfalls we have all experienced in business."

– Asja Svilans, Events & Operations Lead, SPARK Deakin

"This book has opened my eyes to how I can turn my business around. It is the game-changer I need, and I am so excited to put in place the tools I have learned from this inspiring read."

– Pauline Slepoy, Co-founder, My Career Angels

"This book has been extremely insightful and has provided me with many tools that I can use to ensure a successful start to my business."

– Natasha Slepoy-Azimov, Co-founder, My Career Angels

"This is a must-read for first-time entrepreneurs; it offers clear, concise and actionable insights that can be applied to achieve real outcomes in the real world."

– Ashwin Ramachandran, Co-founder, Sapyen

Acknowledgements

I commenced my journey in life and entrepreneurship learning from two extraordinary people, my parents — Radhika and Kishore Mulchandani. Thank you for spending your lives laying the strongest foundations for us so that we can continue to build on them. This book would not have been possible without your unconditional love and support in every step of my life.

My amazing husband, Jaidev Hemnani, who indulges my crazy ideas, encourages me to pursue them and stands proud by my side every single day. Thank you for being my biggest fan and my pillar of strength.

To my brother, Puneet Mulchandani, and my sister-in-law, Anjali Mulchandani, thank you for your love and support always and for bringing my little bundle of joy, Kiara, into this world. There were many days I wondered if this book would make it to the finish line but having her to hug and hold kept me going. I hope one day, when she is old enough to read, this book will nurture the entrepreneurial spirit within her.

My extended family from all over the world, thank you for your constant love, support and encouragement in all my endeavours.

Over the years, I have had the opportunity to work with and learn from some of the most brilliant people on earth. This book would not have come into existence if it weren't for my experiences in corporate, with startups and my education thus far. To those I have worked with, coached, mentored, taught and led, thank you for trusting me to show you the way, for being open and willing to take my advice and for valuing my work. To those that have coached, mentored, taught and led me, thank you for sharing your kindness and wisdom so generously and helping me grow.

Thank you, also, to two incredible women who helped shape this book. My book coach, Kath Walters (and team), for your efficient advice every time and for your patience in working with me. My editor, Lu Sexton, for working your wordsmith magic into my writing.

To the Notion Press team, my publishers, thank you for your prompt responses and follow-ups, and in taking my manuscript and turning it into a tangible book.

My co-founders on various business projects, especially Dario Martinez de Azcona and Laura Galvis, thank you for your support and counsel on our work together. Thank you also for your consent to share our stories openly in this book.

All the wonderful startup founders and entrepreneurs, my colleagues, clients and business friends who agreed to have their stories featured in this book, thank you for sharing your journey with me. Your ideas and experiences inspire me so much.

To all my first readers, thank you for your time and dedication in reading the manuscript. Your insights, feedback and testimonials are invaluable.

To the experts William Siebler and Prasoon Veerath, for lending their time and their specialist skills on the technical areas in this book, thank you so much.

Lastly, my team at Jumpstart Studio, thank you for managing things so autonomously while I chipped away at this book.

Introduction: Start

On a warm Saturday evening in January 2020, as I sat down on my couch to unwind, I got a surprising message on my phone. Michael, a former colleague, was in a reflective mood. After 20 years of working in large organisations in banking, consulting and insurance, he contemplated doing something different. His message said, "Sangeeta, I've been following your business journey on LinkedIn. It's inspiring. I've been thinking about starting a business too, but I wouldn't know where to begin. I wish I could do what you are doing."

There was a vulnerability in that message. I knew that feeling. In 2016, when I first thought about quitting my corporate career to start a business, I found myself stuck in the same spot. I didn't know where to start. I was in a well-paying job, climbing the corporate ladder and getting good at it. But I wasn't happy. I craved something more. I didn't know what to do about it. Who do I turn to? What if I fail? What would people think? What if I lost all my savings? Will I be able to make money? Mortgages, loans . . . what if I can't pay them?

All those fears crippled me. Stopped me from doing what I wanted to do. It took me two years to get over my fears and do something about it — two years that I could have used to get started on my dream instead.

If you are in the same place I was at back then, I am here to help. I don't want you to waste two years wondering and worrying. I want to help you start turning your dream into reality right now.

Many large businesses you see today started in the same place as you and me — with a dream. People who started those businesses also had fears, but they found a way to overcome those fears. This book is going to help you do that. Will it make you a millionaire or give you a billion-dollar unicorn business? It might. But you won't know unless you start. And that is what this book will help you do. Start.

So many people wait for the perfect time, the perfect environment, the perfect situation before they can do something big — and they never end up doing anything. They reach the end of their lives, look back and have regrets. If my experience has taught me anything, now is the time to do whatever you are thinking of doing.

The Secret of Success

Every day, millions of business ideas are born in the world. But not every idea becomes a successful business. The biggest reason is that no one cares about your clever idea unless it solves something for them. People pay money to have their problems solved, not because they love your idea.

> **Business success doesn't depend on how brilliant your idea is. It depends on how you can convert your brilliant idea into a solution for other people.**

The biggest hurdle that early-stage founders must cross is detaching themselves from their idea. Your business is more about your customer than it is about your idea. Founders often think that if they can get even 1% of people in the world to use their idea, it will make them a millionaire. What they don't focus on is how to get that 1% to pay for their idea. And they fall into this deep and dangerous chasm of building something fancy without knowing who is going to buy it. This book shows you how to cross that chasm in the safest and shortest way. In a way that is most likely to succeed.

To be successful in business, every founder must focus on three things — mindset, strategy and execution. Getting these three aspects right will ensure your business has direction, builds momentum and delivers results.

Business Success Framework

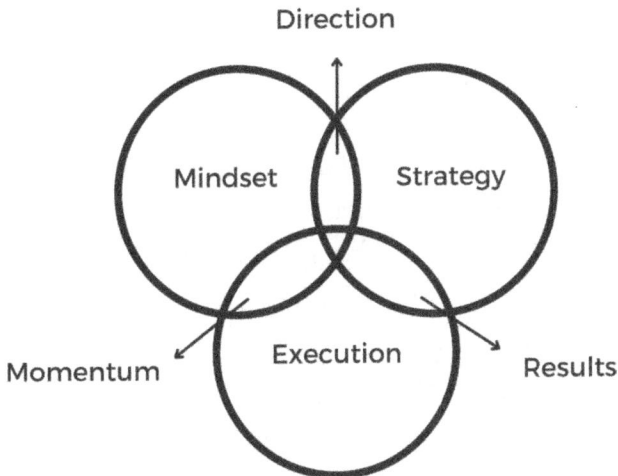

Direction

Mindset

Strategy

Momentum

Execution

Results

Of these three, mindset is the most important piece — it drives your attitude and the way you approach your business. So that's where this book starts.

- Part One will help you get into the right mindset for business with specific exercises for you to do.
- Part Two will show you how to set out a strategy for your business that will give you direction and clarity.
- Part Three will get you to execute that strategy in a step-by-step and modular fashion, to create momentum and deliver outcomes.

Why me

I was born and raised in a business family in India. I watched my parents go through the ups and downs of owning and operating their own businesses. My mother, a serial entrepreneur with an innate knack for business, started her business journey at 31 after having two kids and never having worked before. She stuck her fingers in many pies and ended up with a successful chain of bespoke clothing and apparel manufacturing stores. My father started his business in electronics at 21 and stuck to his one true love for 42 years and counting. We often joke in the family that for Dad everything else comes second, even Mum.

I took a different route though. For 14 years, I worked with large global organisations like Lufthansa Airlines, Ernst & Young and ANZ Bank in roles across finance, IT, risk, operations, sales and senior leadership. While big business excites me, I always found the entrepreneurial journey fascinating. So in 2018, I gathered the courage to pursue my own entrepreneurial journey. I took a break from my corporate career the following year and spent it studying an intensive Master's in Entrepreneurship from Wade Institute of Entrepreneurship, Melbourne Business School, and University of Melbourne. And I started building my own businesses.

My first one, a travel business, failed. Then, I co-founded a food business. It got impacted by the COVID-19 pandemic and got shelved. My third one, in strategy and leadership consulting, was started in the middle of the pandemic. By then I was in love with the entrepreneur in me. I decided to quit my corporate career to focus on my business. As it started stabilising, I started my fourth one, Jumpstart Studio, where I mentor professionals and first-time founders to turn their brilliant ideas into reality and build profitable businesses. As I write this book, I am laying plans for my fifth one with my co-founder.

The more I give into the entrepreneurial process, the more I get from it. I'm a speaker, mentor, guest lecturer and judge at many startup and innovation programs at the University of Melbourne, Deakin University and RMIT. I feel honoured and humbled to have the opportunity to work with hundreds of founders and businesses, from different industries and walks of life, to help them step into their full potential and achieve their dreams.

In this book, you will find stories and lessons from some of the greatest thinkers and doers I have met. You will learn from my own mistakes and experiences, and from the journey of other startups and businesses I work with.

If you have the desire to start and build a business of your own, this book is for you. If your own fears cripple you and stop you from getting started, this book is for you. If you want to learn the shortest and surest way to make your business ideas a reality, this book is for you. If you've taken the leap already but are struggling and not sure how to make it work, this book is for you.

> **The purpose of this book is to be your guide and best friend in your business journey. It's your roadmap to the profitable and successful business of your dreams.**

Let's do it!

PART 1

MINDSET

Chapter One

Find Your Sweet Spot

Did you know that almost half of the businesses that fail make the same mistake?

They build something nobody wants.

In 2017, an analysis on 101 failed startups by CB Insights, published by Forbes Statista, found that 42% of businesses failed because people didn't want to buy what they made. The second biggest reason for failure was financial mismanagement — 29% of businesses said they ran out of cash. So how do you avoid becoming a part of those two statistics?

Ideas don't cost you a penny, but neither do they make you a dollar. Most founders think having a great idea will make their business successful. This could be true to some extent. Ideas, however, don't matter unless you can convert them into profitable businesses. You might think all it takes is some strategy and execution to make your ideas a reality. But there is one step you must take before that: setting up your mindset for success. This begins by identifying which idea is worth converting into dollars and which ideas you must abandon, as alluring as they may be.

Not every idea you have can become a business. Picking the right one is key. When starting a business for the first time, this might seem like a hard task to do, but it is possible. In startup language, it's called ideation. Ideation is not just generating a heap of ideas and picking the one you like best. There are two stakeholders to satisfy when ideating — yourself and your customer. If you start a business based on an idea that you think is great but nobody else does, you may fail. This chapter will show you how to start picking ideas that have a higher chance of success.

Eric Ries, an American entrepreneur and the author of *The Lean Startup: How Constant Innovation Creates Radically Successful Businesses,* says, "The goal of a startup is to figure out the right thing to build, the thing that customers want and will pay for, as quickly as possible."

Just because your idea is brilliant, it's not enough to make your business work. If you ever wonder why some people become super successful at their business and many others fade away without even a mention, it's because successful people pick the right ideas. Ideas that work for them and their customers.

It takes many things for a business to succeed, and the two most important things are you and your customer. Understanding who you are and why you want to build a business — and knowing how to align it with who your customer is and what their needs are — will be the two most important factors in determining the success of your business.

The real currency

Just as a business idea won't get you customers, starting a business won't either. There are steps you must take between your idea and getting your first profitable customer. I'm not talking about the obvious logistical steps like registering a business name, getting specialists like lawyers and tax accountants onboard. There are millions of books about that. Neither am I talking about becoming a super-successful unicorn business, with a valuation of over a billion dollars overnight. You will get there over time. I'm talking about understanding how you can convert your ideas into reality within the next few weeks to attract your first profitable customer.

> **The secret is to uncover what the world needs and turn that need into dollars.**

Most founders are obsessed with their ideas. Once they have an idea stuck in their head, they are convinced that it is going to change the world. They start working on their idea with gusto and making sure everything is perfect before they can go out and sell their product or service to the customer. The problem with that is you end up spending time, effort and money on something that you don't know will sell. To make your ideas matter, you must take the customer-first approach. If you have a hundred ideas, I've no doubt that you can build out each one of those hundred ideas. But if you don't have a customer for any of them then you don't have a business. You have a hundred hobby projects.

The main difference between a hobby and a business is money. Having a hobby is fine if that's what you want it to be. Many businesses start out as hobbies, which is a great way to test the market.

Facebook started as a hobby in 2003, called Facemash. According to the student newspaper, *The Harvard Crimson*, Mark Zuckerberg created Facemash as a fun project to compare online photos of different students at the university. Within the first four hours online, Facemash attracted 450 visitors and 22,000 photo views. However, the Harvard administration team deemed the project unethical and shut it down.

This hobby project became the inspiration for Facebook, the popular social media and networking platform we know today. In the following year, Zuckerberg incorporated Facebook. As universities didn't have online student directories, Facebook addressed this need in the market. I'm sure you know, today Facebook generates revenue from companies that want to access millions of users on the platform. Facemash was not a business idea; it was a hobby that turned out to be a great testing ground for a business. You will learn more about testing the market for your ideas in Chapter Seven. For now, the first thing to do is a reality check about your business idea. Is it a hobby or can it become a business? Is it solving a need that you can convert into dollars?

EXERCISE 1: IDEATE

1. List your ideas

Make a list of all the business ideas that you have today and identify who will pay you money for each idea when it becomes a reality. You don't need specific names of people but a high-level understanding of age groups, gender and location of people who you anticipate would buy from you.

2. Rank your ideas

Once you identify possible customer groups for your idea, start ranking your ideas. Rank them based on two key factors:

- ◆ Do people need it?
- ◆ How unique is this idea?

You could have a unique idea, but people may not need it. Or you could have an idea that many people need, but it's not unique. It's already available in the market and there's competition out there. That's okay. You will learn more about how to deal with competition in Chapter Four. For now, rank your ideas based on your knowledge of the market and your knowledge of potential customers for your idea. You could use a table to capture this activity, like in the example below, which is ranked from one to three, with one being high need or uniqueness and three being no need or not unique. You will use the information here in the rest of this chapter and in the rest of this book.

Idea	Possible customer	Ranking based on need	Ranking based on the uniqueness
Holiday retreat for pets	Pet owners based in Australia	3	1
Solar water heaters	Homeowners, 30–60 years old	1	3
Toy library for kids	Parents of kids aged 6–10 years old	2	2

Turn passion into a possibility

When I started my first business, I wanted to do something I was passionate about. I thought it would give me a higher chance of success. I love travelling. It is one of my biggest passions. I've visited 40 countries and have lived and worked in many of them.

In 2017, I did a 12-month program with a remote-working company called Remote Year. Participants in their program travel and work for 12 months, in groups of 50 to 75 professionals, spending each month in a different country across the world, to live and experience these countries like locals. It was one of the best experiences of my life. I wanted to make this experience-based travel accessible for more people — people who can't commit to travelling for a whole year but can live the same experience for one to two weeks at a time.

I was very excited by the concept and spent many nights and weekends setting up the business — identifying the locations, working out the logistics, finding and negotiating with vendors, setting up a website, sorting out payment systems and testing the market once everything was ready. Soon I realised that while I liked planning my own travels, I didn't enjoy managing travel logistics for others. I'm a great consumer of travel, but not a good producer of it for others. Although I had put in a lot of time, effort and money into building out this travel business, the more I tested the idea, the more I realised it was just not going to work for me. I discovered that what I enjoy about travelling was the opportunity to meet people from different cultures, build relationships and learn from them, not the logistics side of it. I then reflected on other areas in my life — my work, education, personal life. I started seeing a pattern: variety, change and learning new things kept coming to the surface as common themes and drivers.

Business is a long-term game and focusing on the wrong things can lead to a very unhappy journey. It became clear to me that my travel business, although based on my passions, wasn't going to succeed because it didn't align with my internal drivers. I failed at my first business. But I learned a valuable lesson.

Passion is a great place to start when thinking about your business ideas. But take the time to understand what you love about your passions. Don't be too literal in choosing the focus of your business. Go beyond the passion itself to distil and identify underlying and intangible drivers.

Get to the root of what drives you and keeps your momentum going. Use these drivers to build something you love doing day in and day out. If you take your passion as is and make it into a business, it will become a chore and you will lose the magic of what you love about it. Instead, turn your passion into a possibility.

EXERCISE 2: PICK YOUR PASSIONS

This exercise can save you from going down the wrong rabbit hole as I did.

1. List your passions

List your top three passions or things that give you absolute joy and pleasure. If you don't know what they are, answer the following questions which will help you identify your passions.

i. If you had all the money in the world, what would you spend your time doing?

ii. What do you do today that gives you a deep sense of fulfilment and happiness?

2. Answer these questions

For each of these passions, answer these three questions:

i. How does it make you feel? Describe what you feel when you do that activity or that action. For example, when I travel to a new country, I feel free and excited to explore the unknown.

ii. What makes you do it repeatedly? For me, it is the variety, the change and the opportunity to learn during my travels that makes me seek out the experience over and over.

iii. What would stop you from doing it? In my case, if travel did not involve the opportunity to expand my horizons or meet new people and share experiences with them, I wouldn't do it.

3. Repeat and reflect

Do this exercise for three or more passions. You will see some commonalities come through. Identify three to five commonalities. Now reflect if you see these in other areas of your life too — at work, your education, your personal life. Your key internal drivers will become evident.

Your expertise

There are two main reasons most corporate professionals with work experience choose to build a business. One, so that they can quit their jobs. Two, to do something that they love. Often, it's both. However, the various demands of entrepreneurship take a toll. There are many things that you do all by yourself in the beginning as a startup founder. Administrative tasks, marketing, sales, accounting, taxes, hiring people, firing people. Soon, the initial glamour of entrepreneurship washes away and your dreams of freedom come crashing down. You build to-do lists every other day and become focused on execution. You forget to be strategic and just go about doing task after task. You wonder if it is worth it. After all, you didn't get into entrepreneurship to build websites and make Google ads.

The key to being successful at anything is playing to your strengths. Gallup, a well-recognised HR reporting and analysis company, found that people who use their strengths every day have three times better quality of life. In their article from 2015, 'Employees Who Use Their Strengths Outperform Those Who Don't', Gallup found that playing to your strengths makes you six times more engaged at work and 8% more productive.

EXERCISE 3: DEFINE YOUR STRENGTHS

In this exercise, I'd like you to consider everything you have done in your life so far to define your strengths, using a combination of your own self-awareness and the perception of others.

1. List your strengths

Make a list of five to ten strengths that you are aware of. Be clear about them. Know why they are your strengths.

Write two examples of when you have demonstrated these strengths recently. For instance, if one of your strengths is attention to detail, write down two situations when you have displayed this strength in the last couple of months.

2. Ask your close network to name your strengths

Choose ten people who know you very well, family, friends and colleagues. Ask them to describe five things they see as your strengths. Not weaknesses, just strengths. Ask them to give you examples of two situations where they have seen you demonstrate each strength.

Do this exercise via email so that you have a record of their feedback. If writing an email or reaching out to someone is hard for you, start by speaking to people in your immediate family or your closest friends. Most people who interact with you see your strengths in action every day. You will be surprised by how fast they can list them. Write down their answers.

3. Look for themes and refine

Collate all the emails and answers and add them to the list you created. Look for common themes. Identify your five dominant strengths and record them somewhere you can revisit, like a journal.

Once you know your strengths, you know what you are best suited to do. For the other bits, you can always employ people. Playing to your strengths makes sure that you love and enjoy what you do. Don't undervalue the power of that. In the next topic, you will see how to use this information to build your business.

Your sweet spot

An entrepreneur's journey is long and hard. It takes more than just short-term commitment and resilience to get across the line. But it can also be very enjoyable.

To make your business dreams come true, you must:

- love what you do
- be great at it
- align with what the world needs.

This brings together all the things that we've looked at in this chapter so far. When you combine external success factors (what the world needs) with your own internal success factors (your strengths and the drivers behind your passion), you will find your sweet spot. This is the foundational axis that you can build your successful business on.

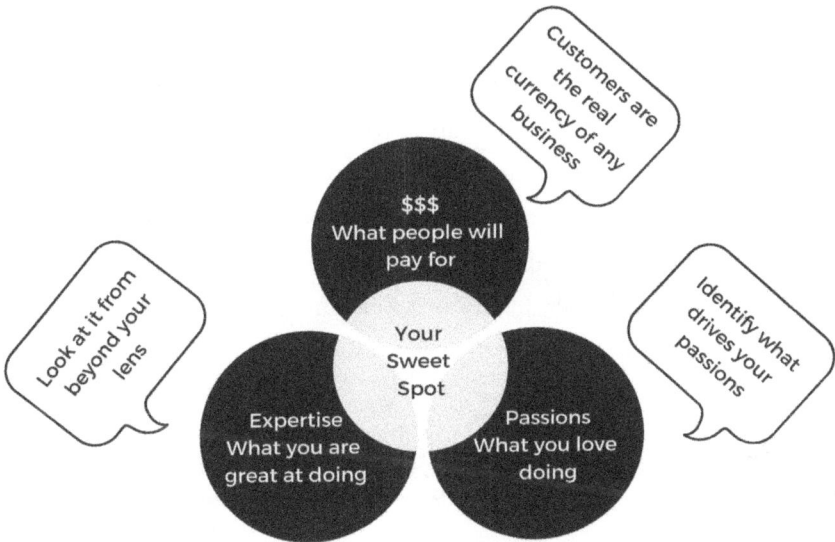

Entrepreneurship is so much more than just a way to replace your income and your day job, it is a journey. If you don't understand this, you may struggle. If your primary goal is income replacement, I recommend you look for investment opportunities instead of starting a business. Yes, your business must reap the financial rewards for your efforts. However, the primary purpose of your business must be to solve people's needs and help you achieve your dreams of freedom. Therefore, it's imperative that you find your sweet spot. This will allow you to build a sustainable business that gives you the rewards that a business should.

Since 2019, I've done several experiments and tested out many businesses to identify my sweet spot. Had I identified it earlier, it would have saved me a lot of time, energy and money. But the silver lining is that every venture helped me learn more about myself and what other people needed. It led me to the work I do today with my consulting clients and first-time founders, which is a good balance between my internal drivers and customer needs.

I've combined those three things — my strengths, my internal drivers and what the world needs. Helping other people create businesses is exciting because it gives me the opportunity to work across new business ideas with a range of different people. It's the perfect fit to my internal drivers such as variety, change, learning and success. It also lets me play to my strengths of strategy design, big-picture thinking and rapid execution. Since the onset of COVID-19, many people want to change careers, to do something more purposeful and start their own businesses. But they don't know how or find it too hard and risky to start something new. This is the key customer need I solve and get paid for — showing people how to start a successful and profitable business. Combining these three aspects gives me a great sweet spot.

EXERCISE 4: FIND YOUR SWEET SPOT

To identify your sweet spot, use the three activities we've done so far in this chapter. Put them on a single page and you will start seeing your external and internal success factors together.

1. Pick the top three from the list of business ideas you ranked by customer need and uniqueness.

2. Choose your top three to five internal drivers.

3. Add your five dominant strengths to the list.

When you put them all on one page, you will see a full and refined view of your success factors. You will be able to identify your sweet spot. When you base your business idea on your sweet spot, you will have the best chance of success.

If you find that multiple ideas fit in your sweet spot, that's okay. You will see how to narrow down to one in Chapter Three.

Entrepreneurship is not just for the chosen few

Entrepreneurship is not a gene that needs to be inherited. Anyone can become an entrepreneur. It takes a bit of know-how and a bit of learning along the way. If you're thinking about it, there is no better time than now to start this journey. It's not about becoming an overnight success, but learning the strategies and laying the right foundation to maximise your chance of success. My aim is to show you how to get started on that journey in a way that has a higher chance of success.

There is no one formula to success, but there are skills and behaviours that anyone can learn to build successful businesses. This book will help you learn the strategies to convert your ideas into a profitable business. Without the right strategies and execution to monetise your idea, you will just be building a hobby.

When you first started working, nobody guaranteed your success, but you found your way to where you are today. When you started school, nobody said you were going to finish school or ace it, but you found your way. There are no guarantees in business, but you will find your way. It's about laying the right foundation to give you that maximum chance of success. It's not something that you inherit from anywhere or that somebody gives you. The more you take guidance from people who've walked this path before, and from the examples and stories that I will tell you in this book, the greater your chances are of finding your way to success.

EXERCISE 5: SET YOURSELF UP FOR SUCCESS

Ask yourself these questions to identify the key things that will help you become successful:

1. What do you want to achieve by building a business? List three key reasons for what you want to achieve.

2. Why does each of these achievements matter? What will happen if you don't achieve them?

3. What are five reasons that make you believe achieving these goals is possible?

Now sit back, shut your eyes and imagine yourself one year from now. You've achieved the goals you set out here. You've made your business idea a reality and are building a profitable and successful business. What does that feel like? What do you see yourself doing? Visualising your own success is a significant starting point. It's time for you to put the pieces in place to achieve that success. Build your business because you believe in that vision you just saw.

IN SUMMARY...

- Not every idea can become a business. Not every business will become successful.

- Start by finding out what is important to you and what you can make a business out of. Finding the right business for you, combining both your passion and expertise, along with what the market demands and what they're willing to pay for today, is your sweet spot — the business idea you should pick for a higher chance of success.

- Rather than obsessing about ideas, focus on what your customer needs. Find your sweet spot, keeping the customer in mind.

- Once you've determined where you want to go, it's time to prepare yourself for the journey. It's like going on a long road-trip. Pack everything that you need for now. And you'll pick up more stuff along the way.

Chapter Two

Embed Safety Nets

I grew up in a city called Coimbatore, which is located in the south of India. Everyone who worked in my immediate and extended family was in business. Dinner-table conversations revolved around business. From a young age, I would help my mum manage her stores, count and price her inventory, and tally the cash flow. When I started my career in 2006, I worked with large multinational businesses. I worked across different business units and learned a lot about big businesses. So, when I started my own business, I had a fair bit of business experience already. Yet, the biggest learning for me as an entrepreneur has been about changing my mindset. Running your own business requires a certain mindset, one that is different from watching others run a business or being someone else's employee.

Entrepreneurship starts with creating the right mindset to achieve your dreams. It takes more than an idea and willpower. You must condition your mind and your behaviour to be business-ready. I'm not talking about undergoing formal training or education to achieve this. I took that long route and yes, it was beneficial. But the key is to understand how to make entrepreneurship work for you and how to make your ideas work for your customer.

In this chapter, you'll see how you can maximise your experiences from the past to prepare for the future. It all starts by knowing which skills, networks, information and experience you must hold on to and which you must relearn, rebuild or relinquish. I will give you practical strategies on:

- how to develop the right mindset for your entrepreneurial journey
- how to set yourself up for success by becoming fail-ready
- how to build your personal and financial resilience for the road ahead.

Start from one

Most people think switching careers from a corporate job to a business means starting from zero, starting from nothing. But building a business is not about reinventing the wheel; it's about leveraging.

Leveraging means taking maximum advantage of something that already exists to speed up what you want to achieve. It means starting from one: the point that you are at today with all your skills, experience, networks and resources. You can use all of it to your advantage when you start your business, even if it is your first one.

If you carry the mindset of starting from one instead of zero, you are bound to create something spectacular. You may need to let go of some specific things from your past, which we will look at later on in this chapter, but to start with, I want you to think about leveraging what you have at your disposal today. Start from one.

EXERCISE 6: IDENTIFY YOUR ONE

These three activities will enable you to identify skills and people that you can leverage when you start your business.

1. Identify your skills, strengths and experiences

A simple way to do that is to update your CV or your LinkedIn profile. It's a great way to refresh your mind about all the different experiences that you've had, as well as all the skills and qualifications that you have. It also gets your profile up to date. You may have worked in a corporate job for ten or twenty years but being able to put it all in one place, to understand and connect the dots on what your different experiences and skills are, is the first step. You could also use some information that you gathered from the strengths exercise in the previous chapter.

2. Update your network list

If you don't have a list of all your networks in one place, create one. You can use Microsoft Excel or Google Sheets to create this online. List all the reliable people you know in your network, people you've worked with in the past, people you have a good relationship with. Don't list somebody you've just met once and don't intend to meet or contact again. Ideally, this list should include at least 20 people. They can be colleagues, family and friends. List where they are today and what they do. If you haven't touched base with them in a long time, make the effort to get in touch with them. Keep your network alive. In business, as in a corporate career, it is who you know that matters more than what you know.

3. Identify current or potential industry bodies

List any industry bodies that you are a part of, or can be part of, based on your current situation as well as the future business that you want to build. For example, this could be the local business network in your area or an association for specialists in your current industry.

Unlearn to relearn

When I met Leena for the first time in 2020, she was on the verge of leaving her corporate job and starting her own career-coaching business. A Human Resources (HR) professional with 12 years of experience, Leena had worked in a few different countries, including Singapore, Hong Kong and Australia. She wanted to start a business so that she could help more people find fulfilling and satisfying jobs. Her business idea was an app that would help match job seekers with employers. Like Tinder, but for job seekers and employers. If both parties swiped right, she would contact them both and coach the job seeker based on the employer requirements. Coming from an HR background and building a business in the same domain, Leena was leveraging her experiences well. She understood the pain points of the HR teams in organisations, and her idea stemmed from there. However, she didn't have a very good understanding of the job seeker's challenges. When she conducted some research and customer discovery (a concept we will look into in the coming chapters), she uncovered things that she had no clue about before she started. For example, she found that job seekers, while struggling to find jobs, didn't think they needed additional coaching. They also weren't willing to pay for an app when they could apply to jobs for free on other platforms. Leena had to unlearn some of her previous conditioning to be able to help job seekers. She had to stop thinking like an HR professional and had to put herself in a job seeker's shoes. This experience helped her approach her business idea with a renewed curiosity.

Much of what you've learned about business and work comes from your experience. While you must leverage your experience, you must also recognise that some of it must be unlearned. Not to forget what you know, but to make room to learn more. To learn better. It's like going from primary school to high school. At first, some things may seem familiar and some hard to do. But you must build on what you know and discard some of your old beliefs to make room for the new.

Be prepared to unlearn and relearn all at the same time. Recognise what aspects you can carry over from your previous mindset and experience, and what others you must develop to become a successful entrepreneur. Consider the differences between an employee mindset and an entrepreneur mindset. If you have been working for an employer for a long time, making the switch to being your own boss means that your mindset and behaviours will need to shift. Otherwise, you'll be stuck acting as an employee in an entrepreneur's shoes.

EXERCISE 7: EXAMINE YOUR MINDSET

We will look more deeply into cultivating an entrepreneurial mindset though execution in Chapter Five. But for now, consider the differences in employee and entrepreneur mindsets from the list on the next page. Where do you sit?

Employee Mindset	vs.	Entrepreneurial Mindset
1. Role-focussed		1. Business-focussed
2. Task doer		2. Initiative taker
3. Thrives in "busyness"		3. Thrives in learning and doing
4. Limits own responsibility and accountability		4. Looks for new responsibilities and accountability
5. Lives by the rules		5. Makes and breaks rules

Get with the times

One of the most popular ways of doing business in the past was to build your product or service and then try to sell it — the 'build it and they will come' approach. It's what I did with my travel business, remember? To some extent, retail businesses today follow this model. The biggest risk in this model is what if you build it and they don't come? What if you rent a store, stock it with your amazing product and open your doors, but nobody walks in? That was the reality for many businesses that opened shop just before the COVID-19 pandemic. Not many have survived since. For online businesses too, this approach doesn't work. What if you build a fancy, expensive website showcasing your products, engage your supply chain vendors, invest in raw materials and production, but nobody buys?

In 2020, I ran a little experiment to test this. I picked a very popular business model, selling coffee mugs on the e-commerce platforms Etsy and Amazon. When you search for the phrase 'selling mugs on Etsy' on Google, you will find many videos from people who claim they have become millionaires by selling coffee mugs online. So, a few weeks before Mother's

Day, a popular time for people to buy coffee mugs as gifts, I designed 15 different mugs and put them on Etsy and Amazon. I had built my shop on these giant e-commerce platforms which had millions of customers come by every day. I'd worked out the keywords, made sure my products featured high on their search pages, and provided all the relevant information necessary. Then I waited for some of these millions of customers to come to my shop.

Mother's Day came and went. I sold zero mugs.

You could blame it on my design skills, but there was more at play here. The experiment proved that it's not about waiting for your customers to come to you. It's about asking, 'why will they come to you?' When there are so many others providing them the same thing that you are providing, why will they come? Why should they choose you over other options? It also shows that just starting a business won't make it successful. There are certain strategies and techniques, which you will learn more about in the rest of this book, that will make your business succeed.

Gone are the days of 'build it and they will come'. Whether you are starting a brick-and-mortar business or an online business, the new mantra is 'sell it before you build it'. Take the customer-first approach. Ask them what their needs are and figure out how you can build a solution. Setting up shop and hoping customers will come is not a good enough business model. I don't mean you shouldn't set up shop at all, but do so after you've got the customers. Create demand before you create supply. To do this, you'll need a functional business model, which you will learn more about creating in Chapter Three and beyond.

Learn from what businesses in the past have done, but don't be a slave to it. If you do what you saw your parents and older generations do, you will soon become irrelevant. You may still choose the same industries and keep some of the valuable traditions, but also learn to do things that are geared for today and the future. Leverage what works but also recognise that the world is changing around you. The business you set up today must flow with the times. This ties back to the very essence of this book — laying the right foundations for your business. The world around you is changing fast. For example, COVID-19 has disrupted even the simplest of routines like going to the office or meeting people. Most people have adapted well to working from home. This has changed the way so many businesses, like cafes and restaurants that rely on office goers as their primary customers, do business. The ones who were able to adapt, survived. The others couldn't.

So, make sure you know how you will adapt and survive with the times.

EXERCISE 8: GET FUTURE-READY

As you start to build your business, keep these five principles in mind and embed them in your business DNA.

1. Omni-channel

Make sure you can serve your customers on multiple platforms. Businesses with presence on many different platforms like web, mobile and offline create better value for their customers.

2. Data focus

Collect and use relevant customer data to drive the business. Data = facts. Businesses that base their strategies on relevant customer data stay ahead of those that operate based on assumptions.

3. Continuous learning

Use learnings from your business to grow and progress. Learning organisations seek to do things better on a continuous basis and create exceptional value in the market.

4. Ecosystem lens

Consider the whole end-to-end ecosystem in which you operate. One of the fastest ways to achieve growth is by working in tandem with the business ecosystem you operate in. Consider opportunities to co-operate, collaborate and partner where you can.

5. People-centricity

When people in your business thrive, the business thrives. Create an environment that supports your three stakeholder groups: employees, customers and shareholders. (Team building and stakeholder management are massive topics that I help founders with, but it is beyond the purview of this book. It warrants a whole other book.)

Become fail-ready

In 2005, Stewart Butterfield, the founder of the image-sharing app Flickr, sold his business to Yahoo! for $35 million. In 2009, he started his second venture, TinySpeck, which was developing a video game called Glitch. The team that built Glitch was based in different locations and found it hard to communicate. So, while they developed Glitch, they also created an internal communication tool called Line Feed to interact with each other. Butterfield raised US $16 million in 2010 and 2011 for Glitch, but when it launched, the game failed to attract customers and was shut down in 2012. After some deliberation, the team changed their focus to Line Feed. They felt like they had built a communication tool unlike any other in the market. They changed their business model and, in the following year, launched their communication tool as a product in the market. They called it Slack, which has become a huge success as a communication and information sharing tool for teams in organisations. In 2020, Slack was valued at $27 billion. The team behind Glitch took their failure and converted it into success with Slack. They learned from their failure and leveraged what they had to create their own success. They didn't let failure stop them.

Failures, limiting beliefs, days of nothing, questioning why you ever chose to walk this path — these are all the realities a first-time founder faces.

Brace yourself and build a fail-ready mindset to deal with it. Everything in life that hasn't been done yet has a 50% chance of success and a 50% chance of failure — every idea, every dream — but you must keep going.

Most people think an entrepreneur's journey is a smooth line upwards. The reality is that, like everyone else, entrepreneurs also go through many ups and downs in their business.

Entrepreneurial Journey

Expectation

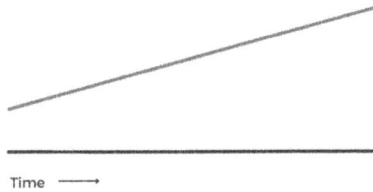

Time ⟶

Reality

Time ⟶

Preparing for failure is as necessary as preparing for success. Failure is labelled as such when you stop doing anything after it. If you keep going after a failure and keep building over it, it becomes a learning experience. To climb the next step in the ladder, there's always learning that needs to take place. To be a successful entrepreneur, you must fail. Without failure, success doesn't have any meaning or value. Every entrepreneur will fail, but how you rise from the failure will determine your success. The risk of not embracing failure is that you will never become successful. And I know that's not what you want.

EXERCISE 9: BECOME FAIL-READY

There are two things you must do to become fail-ready.

1. Be aware of your own limitations and limiting beliefs

Use this list below to identify what holds you back the most. Rank this list with your biggest challenge at the top. When you have identified the top three — ask yourself what you can do to change it or how you can find an antidote for your limiting beliefs. For example, if one of your top three challenges is lack of confidence, ask yourself what will help you become more confident. Who can help you get there? What can you do today to feel more confident — maybe get a haircut, talk to one new person every day or do an activity outside of your comfort zone? It doesn't have to be business related. Once you improve on your limitations in other areas in life, that mindset and attitude will flow into your business decisions.

a. Fear of failure

b. Fear of competition

c. Not knowing how to do something

d. Fear of the unknown

e. Lack of money

f. Fear of instability in your career

g. Fear of not making money

h. Worry about impact to your reputation

i. Lack of confidence

j. Lack of support from family/friends

2. Appoint your personal board of directors

You may have heard of large companies having a board of directors. Likewise, we as individuals also can and must have a board of directors.

This can be made up of people who are our biggest fans, who support us and guide us in different ways.

Find the right people to stand by your side, even if they are not an active part of your business. Whether you have a co-founder or you are starting alone, building a business will come with its challenges. You will need to talk to people through this journey. Draw up a list of 5-7 people from your family, friends, mentors, coaches and well-wishers who can be a great source of strength and support. Ask them if they would like to be on your personal board in a formal capacity. Every time you hit a low or feel like you are failing, call on them to help build you up. They will always know how to put you back on the right track.

You may be wondering if it's a good idea to let other people in on your business. What if they steal your idea? The reality is, not many people have the courage to do what you are doing. Moreover, this is not their sweet spot. You may also think you don't want to lean on others or take help from them. But remember, no successful business has ever been built on the shoulders of a single person. It takes a village to make a business successful. So, make sure you talk to your personal board of directors often about your business and bring them along on this exciting journey with you.

Money matters

Do you know that 77% of people who start their business use their own personal funds to do so?

In 2018, Lendio, a US-based small-business finance lender, found that most of the founders prefer bootstrapping their business. Bootstrapping is the term used to describe businesses that are funded by the founder with no external investment from lenders or investors. Most early-stage businesses will need to bootstrap. It has a lot of advantages, which I will explain further in Chapter Ten, but it also comes with risks.

As you have seen so far, a lot of the mindset work is creative. Most early-stage founders get caught up in the excitement of it all and ignore the financial management side of things. And you too might wonder why you need to think about this so early in the process. But as you saw in Chapter One, the second biggest reason for business failure is founders running out of money. So, being on top of your money matters is crucial at this stage. Because your money matters.

Money management skills will make or break your business. Even if you're not financially savvy or don't want to admit that money makes the world go round, you must get good at managing your money. You don't need to be an accountant or have deep financial skills, but knowing what you need and what you can afford to use and lose is a good start. To do this, you need to get on top of your financial runway. This means knowing how much money you have today and how much money you can afford to use for the business, and being clear about the cut-off point where you can no longer afford to keep going with your business. Always set aside some contingency funds so that you don't run yourself and your family into the ground. Find creative ways to keep the cash flow going until you can create enough cash flow from your business.

Knowing your money matters well gives you a grip on your finances and your lifestyle. It is like building muscle; the more you get involved in managing your money, the better you will get at it. If you choose to ignore your money matters, you risk going bankrupt.

EXERCISE 10: KNOW YOUR FINANCIAL RUNWAY

You can use a simple formula to calculate your financial runway. I'll give you an example on the next page.

Current savings = $25,000

Contingency funds (savings to be retained) = $15,000

Available savings = ($25,000 - $15,000) = $10,000

Cash flow every year (salary, other income sources) = $130,000

Total expenses every year (including rent, mortgages, loans,

living expenses) = $110,000

Available cashflow per year = ($130,000-$110,000) = $20,000

Total available funds = $10,000 + $20,000 = $30,000

Business expenses expected = $2,000 per month

Business runway = $30,000/$2,000 = 15 months

- In this example, your runway is 15 months. This means you have the funds available to sustain your business for a year and three months, just from one year's worth of current cash flow and current savings.

- Your goal must be to generate cash flow from your business within this time if you intend to bootstrap your business and not take on any additional external funding.

- Your runway may increase if you lower your business expenses per month or increase your cash flow from other income sources. When that happens, recalculate your runway to know where you stand.

IN SUMMARY . . .

- Mindset is the starting point for any entrepreneur. Your mindset about learning, failure, preconceptions and money will be challenged when you start your business. View it as a journey and you will see how you are moving up to the next level.

- Like every change you make in life, don't discard your previous learning — leverage it. But also be prepared to upgrade your thought process. Unlearn some of your old beliefs to relearn with curiosity.

- There will be pitfalls along the way, so be ready to fall and rise again many times. Entrepreneurship is as much a journey of personal growth as it is of financial and career freedom, so carry a forward-looking outlook. Don't forget to check your current realities and be prepared for what is to come your way. Put things in place before you head out on the journey and build your self-awareness and financial awareness.

- Once your head and heart are ready to start on this rollercoaster ride, it's time to chart out your strategy to make it happen.

RESOURCES

You can find the following resources from this chapter on my website www.jumpstartstudio.com.au

- Entrepreneurial Mindset Quiz
- Financial Runway Calculator

PART 2

STRATEGY

Chapter Three

Nail the Basics

Amazon has a unique way of developing new products. In 2012, Ian McAllister, the former Director of Delivery Experience at Amazon, revealed that they use a method called 'working backwards'. On a popular online forum, Quora, McAllister says that working backwards at Amazon starts with the product manager writing an internal press release, announcing the finished product. No, they don't have a product yet, it's all in someone's head. It's a vision. But they write a press release as though they've already finished the product, as though they're announcing it to their customers. The content of the press release centres on the customer's problems, the inadequacy of the current solutions and how the new product will be better. This press release is then rewritten, over and over, until the benefits of the new product are distinctive enough to warrant the building of the product. They do this because it's much cheaper to iterate on paper than to iterate on the product itself. It's all about working backwards from the customer rather than starting with an idea and trying to bolt customers onto it.

This process reflects the essential three foundation pillars of any business, which are:

- a clear vision
- a defined set of values
- a robust business model.

The vision for the product becomes clear through the iterative process. Amazon's customer-centric values are demonstrated during the process and become their guiding light. This leads them to developing a robust business model that works for them and their customers.

Vision, values and business model act as anchors for the short-term and long-term goals of your business.

- Without a vision, you don't know where you are headed.

- Without defined values, your decision-making is flawed.

- Without a business model, you don't have a plan to satisfy your customers or a roadmap to make money.

It's not rocket science, but many startup founders fail to establish these fundamental foundations, let alone nail them. In this chapter, you'll establish your business foundations — your vision, values and business model. You will download your ideas on paper before you execute. This is the starting point of your business strategy. It is an initial business plan.

No, not that traditional 100-page business plan on a template you've downloaded off the internet or been handed by a professional. We are taking the startup route, remember. Before you waste your time and energy on a 100-page business plan, you first need to know if your idea has any legs. Do your customers care about your idea? Can you deliver?

All you need at this stage is two pages that define your vision, your values and unpack your idea into a business model. And then, as you go through the remaining chapters of this book, you will start working backwards. To iterate and refine. To test and learn.

Working backwards ensures that you're working towards your vision.

Vision

Working backwards in business starts by thinking big. The easiest way to think big is to ask the question 'what if'. Your vision is about that deep desire that you want to turn into a reality. I don't mean small goals that you can achieve in the next few months. I'm talking about the big dreams that will take you ten or more years to achieve. It's the big change you want to create to make this world a better place. That is your vision.

An entrepreneur's journey has many twists and turns. A big vision inspires you to act in times of despair, to deal with all the risks that you will take as an entrepreneur. It keeps you going when things get tough. It's the fuel to your fire.

Every successful business out there today started with a vision. A vision of purposeful change. Nike, one of the biggest sportswear brands, aspires to bring inspiration and innovation to every athlete in the world. To them, every person with a body is an athlete. In 2021, that is eight billion people. That is a big vision.

A strong and bold vision acts like a magnet. It attracts people — employees, customers and investors — who align with your vision. It makes working backwards easier too. Setting up an organisation, attracting talent, building teams, creating the right products, sourcing money to build your business, all become easier.

However, just having a vision in your head is not good enough. You must be able to communicate that vision to the world on all the different platforms you intend to be on. To do this, you will need a vision statement.

A well-articulated vision statement creates clarity for your business. It's the 'why' behind what you do.

- Why do you exist as a business?
- Why should people work for your business?
- Why should customers buy from your business?

It tells the world what you're trying to achieve — that dream you want to turn into a reality.

Reflect on a vision or mission statement that you have seen before. Does your current employer have one? Does it inspire you? Does your work align with that vision?

EXERCISE 11: CREATE YOUR VISION STATEMENT

Many people struggle to create their vision statement in the early stage of their business. Doing a thought chain exercise can be very helpful. In this exercise, you identify multiple 'what if' statements and link them like a chain. Use your life experiences to reflect on things that matter to you.

1. Create a thought chain about an issue that's important to you

Start with a big, bold statement and go down that chain of thought.

For example:

- What if there is no poverty in the world? Can you close your eyes and imagine a world like that? Does it inspire you? Does it make you happy? If yes, keep drilling down further.
- What if no person went to bed hungry?
- What if all the food we have in the world was available to every person in the world?

2. Create more thought chains

Choose different issues that inspire you to create change. Remember to make them about issues and problems that you care about. The driving force behind your vision is your why. Knowing your why makes your vision statement valuable and sticky, something that stays with you for a long time. Why is it important to you? Why is it important for others — your customers and the world? With the why behind it, your vision becomes more than just a static statement. If you don't know why you're doing something, you're no better than a machine.

3. Find the 'what if' question that fits with your sweet spot

Revisit your sweet-spot ideas from Chapter One. Do any of the ideas fit into any of your thought chains? Do they lead up to a big, bold 'what if' statement?

4. Create your vision statement

Once you've identified the idea that fits both your sweet spot and your thought chain, it's time to create your vision statement. Go to the biggest and boldest 'what if' statement in the thought chain you've picked — 'What if there is no poverty in the world?' Replace 'what if' with 'our vision is' and refine the question into a statement — 'Our vision is to end poverty in the world.' This is your vision statement.

5. Evaluate the statement

Ask yourself, 'How important is this vision to me?' Evaluate it on a scale of one to ten, ten being the highest. And if it's not a ten, go back to the start and do the exercise again.

For example, Google's aim is to organise the world's information and make it accessible and useful to the whole world. A strong, purposeful statement like this has driven them to becoming the world's largest online search engine in the 21st century. They couldn't have got there if that was not a ten for them. So, find that vision statement that is the most important to you. This is the first foundation pillar for your business.

Remember:

- Make your vision statement big, bold and scary to achieve.
- Keep it simple, clear and succinct.
- Aim to inspire three key groups of people — your customers, your employees, your investors.
- Most important of all, check if it inspires you.
- Make it visible and be proud to talk about it. You must, in due time, be proud to put it on your website and all your business collateral. It must tell the world why you exist as a business and what you're going to achieve. You are making a promise to yourself and the world.

Values

In 2020, I had the opportunity to work with a bright, young, aspiring entrepreneur Diya. Her vision was to make education accessible to every child in the world. It was something close to her heart and she believed in it. But her vision wasn't unique; there were so many other organisations working towards the same vision. How was she going to make her work stand out?

This is where values come in. While your vision is the 'what' and the 'why' of your business, your values drive the 'how'. Just as a person embodies a set of values, a business operates with a set of values. They are the principles that shape your business and its identity.

Values shape the culture of a business. They define key behaviours that people working in the business must demonstrate. They are ingrained in the DNA of the business. When the going gets tough or when you must make tough decisions, your values are your guiding light. Hence, they must be defined early on and laid down as the next foundation pillar of your business.

Values are not a random set of words that you choose from a list. In the startup phase, the business reflects the founder's personal values. As the business grows and changes, business values change. They are refreshed and repurposed. Much like they change when we grow as individuals.

Like a vision and mission statement, most large companies have a well-defined values statement. A good example is the Australian fintech startup, Airwallex, which was established in 2015 to make cross-border payments and financial exchange easier for businesses. In six years, they have grown to 800 employees across 12 international offices. Their vision is to be the global financial cloud to empower businesses to operate anywhere, anytime.

Their six values, which support their vision statement, are clearly listed on their website. Here are three as an example:

1. Customers first: Our customers are why we are here. Knowing them, keeping them and consistently delivering a superior experience are the only ways we can fulfil our mission.

2. Intellectual honesty: We want to constantly seek the truth. To be open, constructive and transparent, approaching every problem with data and facts, not conjecture and opinion.

3. Obsessive curiosity: We always start by asking why and seek to understand. We have a hunger for knowledge, seek challenges that are insatiably interesting and always consider if there are better ideas.

As you can see, their values outline the behaviour they will exhibit, and also things they will not do, in bringing their vision to life.

EXERCISE 12: IDENTIFY YOUR VALUES

As a new business, start with some simple values that resonate with you as a person. Use the list below to pick five or six values that resonate with you the most. Think about the choices you make every day and why, and the values you seek in others too.

List of Values

Accountability	Fairness	Openness
Achievement	Faith	Optimism
Adventure	Fame	Peace
Authenticity	Friendships	Pleasure
Authority	Fun	Popularity
Autonomy	Growth	Recognition
Balance	Happiness	Religion
Beauty	Honesty	Reputation
Boldness	Humility	Respect
Compassion	Humour	Responsibility
Challenge	Integrity	Security
Citizenship	Impact	Self-Respect
Collaboration	Justice	Service
Community	Kindness	Spirituality
Competency	Knowledge	Stability
Contribution	Leadership	Success
Creativity	Learning	Status
Curiosity	Love	Trustworthiness
Determination	Loyalty	Wealth
Excellence	Meaningful Work	Wisdom

- Now define each value you have chosen with an example or a statement as you see in Airwallex's example.

- Even if there are others out there wanting to achieve the same vision as you, your values are your unique advantage. They are the key principles that you will use to guide your actions to achieve your vision.

Business model

So far in this book you've worked on identifying the right idea, getting into the mindset for business and establishing the first two pillars of your business — your vision and values. Now it's time to map your idea out in a structured business model, the third and biggest pillar of your business. This pillar is crucial to how the rest of your business journey will pan out. The business model you lay out in this section of the book will feed into all the actions you take for the rest of the chapters in this book. If you skip this step, you will have no clue if your idea is business-worthy. Are your thoughts coherent? Are you creating the right solution for the right problem? Will people pay you for your idea? My experience from my second business illustrates the importance of this step.

In 2019, I started a business called Foodtropia with two co-founders, Dario, a hospitality expert who owned and operated multiple hotels in Spain, and Laura, an experienced food regulatory affairs specialist from Colombia. The three of us had one thing in common — our love for food and exploring other cultures. At first, our business idea was to develop a platform to help the grandmas in Australia share their cultural knowledge and traditional food with younger people. We would help them host small gatherings in their homes to share their stories and home-cooked meals. Guests would pay to come eat their meals and this could become an income stream for grandmas. Foodtropia would charge a fee per guest and that was our business model in our heads. However, once we laid out the idea in a structured business model framework on paper, we noticed many gaps in our thinking. Did the grandmas want to do this? Will the guests value these experiences enough to pay for them? How much would we charge them? What would it cost us to get the grandmas to host the gatherings? Would they have to be trained and certified in safe food handling practices like chefs do? Were they willing to be trained? There were a lot of unknowns, and we could only hypothesise at that point.

Mapping out our business model on paper showed us that our idea lacked clarity and crucial information. However, the advantage of using a structured approach was that it showed us which parts of the puzzle were missing. It showed us where to focus our efforts and what to look for. It gave us direction. If we hadn't mapped out the business model and jumped straight into execution instead, we would have got lost along the way.

Your business model is the roadmap that takes you from where you are today to where you want to be.

A business model, by definition, answers the question, 'how does your business make money'. The purpose of this first version of your business model is to provide clarity to your thoughts and direction to your next steps. Tools like the Business Model Canvas by the Swiss business theorist and author Alexander Osterwalder, and the Lean Canvas by Ash Maurya, founder of Leanstack and author of *Running Lean*, are popular in the startup ecosystem. These tools help you map out your business model on a single page, but in my experience, they lack an essential factor. So I have developed a template of my own, which is the next exercise.

But before we dive in, keep in mind that this will be a draft business model, a first iteration. It's highly likely that it will change numerous times as you test your ideas and new information comes to hand. Keeping with the roadmap analogy, it's a bit like Google Maps. When real-time traffic data is updated by the Google Maps server, the best route option often changes to help you reach your destination quicker. That's how you must navigate and use your business model. This first version of your roadmap will change. You will discover alternative routes. Be open to it.

With Foodtropia, our business model changed several times. Every time we tested one of our hypotheses, we found new information and insights. As we kept testing the market, most of the sections in our business model changed. The whole problem statement changed. We discovered that grandmas didn't want to cook for strangers or have them visit their homes. We also found that not many homes were of the standard we wanted our customers to enjoy. The solution we had in mind, our business idea, also changed. From a social impact platform, we became a dinner party platform instead. Our customer segment changed. We found that our dinner parties attracted a different customer segment. Our value proposition to the customer changed. I'll tell you more about it in the coming chapters.

EXERCISE 13: BUILD YOUR INITIAL BUSINESS MODEL

From my experience, a business model must answer 12 distinct questions. Use a large whiteboard or an A3 sheet of paper to map out your business model. This will help you see all the segments of your business model in one big picture. It will make it easier to refine your business model as you go through the rest of this book. Use sticky notes or erasable markers where possible to save you the hassle of redoing your business model when things change in the coming chapters.

Divide your whiteboard or A3 sheet into three sections and answer all the questions from the business model framework on the next page. Most of the information at this point will only be a hypothesis — a guess based on what you know now. So, if you have any gaps or can't answer any of the questions, it's all right. Put down your best guess for now. The rest of this book is designed to help you refine and fill the gaps in your business model.

Business Model

SECTION 1 CUSTOMER DESIRABILITY	SECTION 2 BUSINESS FEASIBILITY	SECTION 3 FINANCIAL VIABILITY
a. Customer segment: Who are you building your solution for? **b. Problem statement:** What problem are you trying to solve for the customers? **c. Current solutions:** What does your customer segment currently use or have access to solve this problem? This is the competition that you have in the market today for your business idea. **d. Your solution:** What is your solution for your customer for this problem? **e. Value proposition:** What benefits and value does your solution offer your customer? (Note: this is not the list of features of your product/service. This is the benefit that your customer gets by using your product/service.) **f. Your differentiating factor:** What is something that your competition or other people in the market can't do today? **g. Emotional value:** How does your product/service make your customer feel?	**a. Partners:** Who can you partner with to deliver the solution to your customer? **b. Channels:** How are you going to reach your customer? Through what physical and digital platforms? **c. Execution resources:** What resources do you require to deliver your product/service? Money is one that every business needs. But beyond that, think about what kind of people you need? Do you need an office? Furniture? Computers? Raw materials? Factory equipment?	**a. Revenue:** How do you expect to make money? What products/services will make you money? Consider your answers in the last two sections and calculate a high level $ amount. **b. Costs:** What does it cost you to build this out? Consider your answers in the last two sections and calculate a high-level $ amount.

- This is the first version of your business model. You will come back to this business model often over the course of this book and your business journey.

- Business models are meant to evolve, so be ready to be flexible and change your mind about your business model as you go through the rest of this book. Having this mindset will let you go from a hypothetical to a real, tangible business.

- Knowing that you're not tied to an idea and having the flexibility to move will get your business up and running faster.

- Don't get too attached to the first version of your business model. As you learn more about the market, customer needs and challenges, you will keep tweaking it. It will start to better reflect your customer rather than your idea. We will start with this tweaking process in the next chapter.

What matters in the end is that your vision comes to fruition through the business model. A great way for you to see how this will feel is to write a testimonial for your business from your happiest customer. Imagine a time when you have served your customer and achieved your vision. What would they say about you? Grab your journal and write a testimonial for your business on behalf of your happiest customer. Now go through the rest of this book and make it happen.

IN SUMMARY . . .

- In this chapter, you've designed a runway for your business idea to take off, and you've identified the different pieces that drive a business strategy — your vision, values and the business model. These are the three foundational pillars of any business.

- Now put all the three pillars together on a single piece of paper and do a sense check. Does it all make sense together? Are you excited?

- In the next chapter, you will learn to narrow your focus to achieve results. Having a high-level strategy is a great starting point, but you must create more clarity in your thoughts and direction before you put your plans into action. Being specific and targeted in your actions will give you the power to accelerate your business. So let's get onto it.

Chapter Four

Narrow Your Focus

I have a confession to make.

I am addicted to shiny new gadgets. I spend hours admiring technology products online and every time I go out shopping, I jump at the news of artificial intelligence-powered headphones or augmented reality glasses. I can talk about the latest laptop or smart watch in the market for hours. However, much like you, I don't end up buying every new product I see or like. I wouldn't, even if I wanted to. I may consider buying augmented reality glasses someday, but I would rather spend my money on that new phone with a long-lasting battery. The one I need because mine doesn't last for more than six hours.

People don't pay money to buy a product or a service even if it is something they love or is feature-packed. They pay money to get their problems solved. Customers don't care about your product or service unless it does something for them. They may splurge for a fancy birthday gift once in a while. But people have problems, and they pay for solutions.

In the last chapter, you established the high-level vision for your business using the thought chain exercise. As you will have seen, the thought chain has many related problems under the same vision. All these problems can be tackled in many ways. And all these problems may even affect many different groups of people, some of which you may have already identified in your business model. But the trick to getting a head start in your business is to find that one group of people who is willing to pay you to get that one key problem solved — the magic of one.

Narrowing your focus to one gives you two key advantages. The first — a strategic advantage. Having a single customer and a single problem allows you to test your ideas fast. You may have many ideas for the solution that can be tested out, but they must pertain to a single customer and solve a single problem. If you try to tackle too many problems or too many customer groups at once, chances are you won't get good at any of them. If you cast your net too wide and aim to solve everybody's problem, you will end up solving nobody's problem. You will create products and services that will never sell.

"In business, the power of one may be viewed through a strategy lens. Strategy is about focus and uniqueness," says Professor Ming-Jer Chen from the University of Virginia Darden School of Business. As a leading authority in strategic management, Chen outlines the power of one in his *Washington Post* article, "Case in Point: Using the power of one as a business practice". He says that every situation has trade-offs and choices. How you choose depends on your core values and how you want to fulfil your mission. The power of one allows you to crystallise what is important and make coherent decisions.

The second advantage of narrowing your focus is productivity. Psychologists Mihaly Csikszentmihalyi and Jeanne Nakamura popularised the concept of 'flow'. When you achieve a state of being where you are immersed in the task you are doing and lose sense of time and space, you are in flow. In flow state, your productivity peaks and your distractions fall away. To achieve this high level of productivity, you must focus on one thing at a time. Headspace, a popular meditation app developed in 2010, has a blog on their website about flow. They say, "Achieving a flow state is best accomplished while focusing on one major task that requires a significant portion of brain power. Multitasking would create a web of distractions that make it impossible to achieve flow state." Focusing on multiple tasks can drain your brain and diminish your personal productivity when trying to build a business. Think of a time you were very productive. I'm willing to bet you weren't multitasking.

Narrowing your focus doesn't mean that things won't change. Remember my business Foodtropia from the last chapter? Everything changed. But it changes when you find out new information from the customer. More on that in the next chapter where you will learn to do customer discovery.

In this chapter, you are gearing up for your business adventures. You are creating clarity for your next steps — clarity about the customer, their problem and the value you can create with your solution.

One customer, one problem

Let me tell you a little story that I call the 'suitcase case'. I am invited as a guest judge at several startup pitch competitions in Australia where aspiring entrepreneurs get up on stage and pitch their business ideas to win some funding or support for their business. I assess over a hundred ideas each year at these pitch competitions. A small fraction of them win, but so many others leave a lasting impression. They make excellent case studies for my coaching and mentoring work, and for this book. The suitcase case is one such example.

Imagine you walk into the departures terminal at an international airport. You see an elderly couple walk past. They both have walking sticks in one hand and are holding onto each other with the other hand. As they walk past you, you also see three full-sized suitcases following them, hands-free. They turn into an aisle on their left and the suitcases take a left turn too, right behind them. Self-moving suitcases that follow you everywhere you go. How cool is that!

When this idea was pitched at one of the competitions, I was excited to see more. As a gadget enthusiast and avid international traveller, it got my attention. The aspiring founder then disclosed the problem he wanted to solve. Accessibility issues for senior travellers, people with disabilities and people with injuries. He described how lifting heavy suitcases in and out from cars is an issue for these people. Putting heavy suitcases onto luggage conveyor belts at the airport is another problem. However, the solution he had come up with was a self-moving suitcase. It wasn't a self-lifting suitcase! So, while the idea was cool and fancy, it wasn't a solution to the problem that his customer segment had. In this case, it was an idea that was looking for a problem to solve. It was a retrofitting of the problem to the idea that the founder was in love with.

Most founders with new and exciting ideas run into what I call the retrofitting risk. They fall in love with their ideas so much that they then start looking for problems that their ideas can solve. Even if there are none. They take an ideas-first approach instead of taking a problem-first approach. Without a problem to solve, you get stuck building out ideas that have no value in the market. Creating value means solving a problem customers care about and will pay you for. Don't let your hard work go to waste.

While you may think of many problems, the trick is to focus on one problem and attempt to solve it with one solution at a time. As an entrepreneur, it is up to you to find the best way to solve a problem for a customer segment. Building things is about you, but solving problems is about your customers. Always keep your customer-centric view on to make sure you're solving the right problems with the right solution.

There are significant differences between taking an ideas-first approach and a problem-first approach. Picking the right approach is a strategic decision. It will make the biggest difference in how successful your business becomes in the market.

Ideas-first approach	Problem-first approach
You build a product or service.	You build a solution.
You will need to find customers who like your idea.	Customers are already looking for you and your solution.
Your business is you-centric.	Your business is customer-centric.
You will have to invest significant money upfront to build your product or service.	You can make money every step of the way while building out the solution.

EXERCISE 14: CREATE A PROBLEM STATEMENT

To avoid the risk of retrofitting and becoming another suitcase case, take the problem-first approach. You'll start by creating a problem statement, which will help you think about your customer and their problem together, not in isolation, which in turn will help you narrow your customer segment even further.

1. Create a problem statement

Using the principle of one customer, one problem, look at the customer segment you listed in your business model from the last chapter. Create a problem statement for them using the problem statement template below. If you listed more than one customer segment, create a problem statement for each of them.Ultimately, you will need to narrow it down to just one customer segment.

"Customer segment wants to achieve a specific outcome,

but they have problem/pain point

because barriers exist

which makes them feel negative emotions/behaviour."

Let's say you want to help mothers of young kids who want cheap toys for their kids because they outgrow their toys very fast and it's expensive to keep buying them. Using the template above, you would create the problem statement as:

"Mums of young kids want to access cheap toys for their kids,

but they struggle to find cheap toys

because they must go to multiple places to look for them

which makes them feel frustrated and is time-consuming."

2. Identify your target market

Look at your customer problem and answer these three questions:

   i. Who are you solving for?

   ii. What are you trying to solve?

   iii. What outcome are they looking for?

These three answers combined will narrow your customer segment to reveal your 'target market'.

Let's look at this with the example of the mums looking for toys:

   i. Who are you solving for? Mums of young kids.

   ii. What are you trying to solve? The struggle to find cheap toys as they must look in different places.

   iii. What outcome are they looking for? Access to cheap toys for their kids.

So here, the target market is not just 'mums of young kids,' it's 'mums of young kids who are struggling to find cheap toys.'

- Narrowing your focus on a target market makes it easier to go deeper into solving the problem. It also gives your business a clear identity and attracts the right clients that you want to and can serve. Who you talk to, what you say and how you say it becomes sharper and more targeted.

- The problem you identify must be single and specific. Specificity in the problem drives a higher quality of ideas for your solution. It makes your job easier and faster. It helps you cut out the noise and prevents you from going around in circles. In the example above, the problem is focused on a specific outcome — access to cheap toys. It's not about finding brand-new toys or hi-tech toys. These may end up being related problems to solve later down the line. The specific initial problem and outcome that you are trying to address is easier access to cheap toys.

- Do a take two on your problem statement. Is the problem and outcome specific enough and related? Keep doing this until you are confident that the whole problem statement is coherent and makes sense.

Who is mum?

In our hypothetical problem statement, we want to help mums of young kids. But who is mum? Is she a suburban mother with a partner and four kids or is she a single working mother trying to make ends meet? Getting into the psyche of your customer and understanding who they are is the next step in the process. You are refining it from one customer segment to one customer in the segment.

> **This is your ideal customer who cannot refuse your solution because they are waiting for you to help them solve their problem.**

One of the best ways to identify and relate to your customer is by building a customer profile. In the discipline of design thinking, it's called a 'customer persona'. A customer persona is a detailed profile about your ideal customer from your customer segment. It's the person that you want as your customer and who is more than willing to pay you for the problem you are solving.

Building customer personas is one of the most fun things you could do in your business journey. It's like when you ask a kid about his or her imaginary friend. They get excited and tell you their friend's name, what they look like, who they are, what they say and do. To start building your customer persona, use a picture of your ideal customer. It could be someone you know. A family member, a friend or somebody in your network.

EXERCISE 15: BUILD YOUR IDEAL CUSTOMER PERSONA

Thinking about these five questions will help you build a picture of your ideal customer:

1. Who are they? – Give them a name, age, living situation, occupation, etc.

2. What are they like? – Think about their different personality traits.

3. What are their challenges and needs? – Think about the specific problem that they have and the goals they have that are relevant to them. What could be some of the challenges to achieving the goal? What are their needs?

4. What are some of her internal drivers? – Think about how their living situation, their occupation and their personality traits come into play with this.

5. What may be some opportunities for you to help?

Let's do this using our hypothetical mum from the problem statement in the previous section.

1. Who is she?

Let's say her name is Sara. Use a picture to visualise her.

- She's 37 years of age.
- She lives in Melbourne in a two-bedroom apartment in the city.
- She's married to Jake, who is 40 years old.
- They have a son, Ryan, who's seven.
- She works as a primary school teacher and has 12 years of experience in the primary education sector.
- She earns $85,000 a year and loves her profession.

2. What is she like?

Sara is caring, generous, willing to help and careful with her spending.

3. What are her challenges and needs?

- The goal for Sara, as per the problem statement, is accessing toys for her son at cheaper prices.

- What could be some of the challenges in doing that? Maybe she finds it too expensive to keep buying toys for her son or she has a lack of space and a lot of clutter because she lives in an apartment.

- What could be her needs here? Easy access to toys, ability to borrow and return when she likes, ability to swap toys, home delivery of the toys?

4. What are some of her internal drivers?

- One of her personality traits is to spend less, so she could save money and space.

- As a teacher, she may want a variety of educational and entertainment experiences for her son.

- Or she may want to keep him occupied since she's working.

5. What may be some of the opportunities for you to help?

Possibilities to help Sara with her problem could be a toy library or a second-hand toy store.

Customer Persona

Age: 37
Marital status: married to Jake, 40 years old
Children: one child - Ryan, 7 years old
Location: Melbourne
Occupation: primary school teacher
Earnings: $85,000 a year

Personality traits:
- caring
- generous
- willing to help others
- careful with her spending

Internal drivers:
- save money and space
- variety of educational and entertainment for her son
- keep son occupied since she's working

Challenges:
- accessing toys for her son at cheaper prices
- finds it too expensive to keep buying toys for her son
- lack of space and a lot of clutter because she lives in an apartment

Needs:
- easy access to toys
- ability to swap toys
- home delivery of toys
- ability to borrow and return when she likes

Opportunities to help Sara:
- a toy library or a second-hand toy store

This is how you create a persona. It doesn't have to be perfect just yet. Fill in all the information you think you know today about your ideal customer. You will refine this as you go in the next chapter.

With Sara, you've created a buyer persona, the person who will pay you for your product or service. For most businesses, this may suffice as the person who buys the product or service is the same who uses it. However, in this example, we have a different user — Sara's seven-year-old son, Ryan. So, while you may focus on the buyer persona, create a persona for Ryan as well. Your business must satisfy both the buyer and user needs.

A question I get asked very often is about how to create a persona if you intend to serve businesses instead of direct consumers. Guess what: businesses are also run by people. In this case, where you are intending to be a B2B (business-to-business) operation, find the decision-makers in your ideal customer business, like the CEO or the COO. Create their personas by looking at the problem from the business lens. There is a more detailed example on how you can approach this in the next chapter.

Competition creates value

If I was paid a dollar for every time I hear first-time founders say, "We don't have any competition in the market," I'd have a nice little side income going. The biggest fallacy among new entrepreneurs is that their idea is unique. Hence, they think they don't have any competition. But the narrative changes when you think about your idea as a solution to a problem. Every problem that you can think of is already being solved. Yes, read that again.

In 2020, the world experienced an unprecedented pandemic. COVID-19. Every large economy around the world grappled with this pandemic. Many cities and countries stopped life as usual and went into snap lockdowns. With mandates to stay, work and play at home, new problems cropped up. However, as human beings, we have a great innate ability to adapt. Some people adapt to new situations better than others. But we are primed to adapt. So, when new problems come our way, we find existing solutions to solve these problems. For example, if your idea is to start an online entertainment service for people in lockdown to kill their boredom, you would have to compete against some of the already popular services like Netflix and Amazon Prime — your direct competitors. That's a no-brainer. On the other hand, you would also have to compete against other alternatives that solve the problem of indoor entertainment, like online parties with friends, books, online cooking classes and board games — your indirect competitors. So even in new situations like a worldwide lockdown and with new problems, people will find a way to solve them with existing solutions.

Most founders have a mental block against competition. It scares them, they feel like they can't progress with their ideas and their image of being the first person to solve the problem shatters. But business is not a boxing match with opponents in the ring. Think of it as a team sport where you must partner and learn from your peers.

Having competition is good for two reasons. First, competition validates that the problem you are trying to solve exists and is valuable enough to solve because people are already paying for a solution. Second, competition can help you create better value for your customers. It gives you a first-hand chance to evaluate what works and doesn't work for your customers, which in turn helps you avoid making the same mistakes with your solution as your competition does.

> **Understanding your competition is the key to understanding the unique value you can offer your customer. It helps you create your unique 'value proposition'.**

Understanding your value proposition and comparing with what your competitors are doing in the market can help you understand how you are different in the market. This point helps you tie together the problem statement and the customer segment. For example, at Jumpstart Studio, our value proposition for first-time founders and entrepreneurs is to prevent business failure. We do this by de-risking the business-building process and using proven and tested startup frameworks and methodologies. Like the frameworks you are learning in this book.

The business model you created in the last chapter helps you think about your competition and the current solutions that your customers use. It helps you outline your value proposition and how you think it differs from existing solutions. You are now ready to refine your answers in your business model using the principles from this chapter. After you have narrowed down your focus to one customer and one problem, you can align your solution and value proposition to the customer and their problems using the exercise below. This will not be your final solution but rather the starting point to test your idea.

At this stage, you are creating initial clarity around your solution and value proposition. As you test out your business model hypotheses in the next few chapters, this will help you gain more meaningful testing outcomes. This is your version one hypotheses, the starting point from where you will begin.

EXERCISE 16: IDENTIFY YOUR VALUE PROPOSITION

In this exercise, you will use your problem statement to identify one or two competitors, what they do to solve your customer's problems, and align your value proposition to the customer's needs, challenges and emotions.

1. Deconstruct the problem

Break down your problem statement into these four parts:

- outcome desired
- problem
- barrier
- feeling.

2. Identify how your competition addresses each of these parts

They may be better at some than others.

3. Identify how you can address them

This is the value you create — your value proposition.

Let's look at this using our toy library example:

Customer's problem	Who is the competition & what do they do?	What value can you create?
Outcome desired: Access to cheap toys for their kids	Toy stores: Sell toys at full price/sale Other toy libraries: Low-cost but tedious process to go there physically	Low-cost toy library or toy swapping service
Problem: Struggle to find cheap toys	**Toy stores:** Inform about discounts **Other toy libraries:** Offer physical catalogues to browse	Make it easy to find toys online on a website or a mobile app, with filters and sorting abilities
Barrier: They must go to multiple places to look for them	**Toy stores:** Categorise their shelves **Other toy libraries:** You need to search physically in the library	Offer home delivery and push notifications about new toys based on preference
Feeling: Frustrated and that it is time-consuming	**Toy stores:** Staff available to help **Other toy libraries:** Staff available to help	Ease the process by making it a recurring service/subscription, and make it less time-consuming by suggesting toys based on previous preferences

IN SUMMARY . . .

- The magic in business starts when you focus and get specific in your approach. When you stop thinking about ideas and start developing solutions to real problems, you gain immense clarity in your thoughts, which gives you a great strategic advantage.

- Narrow your thinking and get specific about who your customer is. Identify the one key problem that is worth solving for your customer.

- Once you have defined your problem statement, your customer persona, and identified the value you can create, you are ready to move to the next chapter.

In the next chapter, I will reveal a secret. It's the single most powerful habit that you and your business must cultivate to become successful, a habit which sets great businesses apart from the average ones — talking to your customers.

RESOURCES

You can find the following templates from this chapter on my website www.jumpstartstudio.com.au

- Problem Statement
- Customer Persona

PART 3

EXECUTION

Chapter Five

Talk to Your Customers

In 2020, in the middle of the pandemic, William, a 32-year-old user experience (UX) designer, found himself without a job. William didn't know what to do next. He started applying for jobs as most people do. But with the job market looking bleak, he had to find a way to make some money to survive. So he started a little business. William saw that people who had a soda-making machine at home got their gas refills at a nearby stockist. They would drive to their stockist with their empty gas cylinders and buy filled ones. It was an expensive and time-consuming process. As a UX designer and with a deep interest in sustainability for future generations, William saw the whole process from the customer's lens. He redesigned the process so that customers could place an order for soda gas cylinders online, via Facebook. William would then deliver filled cylinders in exchange for their empty ones. He could then refill the empty cylinders at home and deliver them to the next customer. This way, he could keep the costs low and pass on the savings to his customers. It also created less waste in the ecosystem.

Soon William's business was competing head-on with some big names in the industry. His little business did what the big businesses couldn't. Create value through customer experience. William redesigned an existing process with the customer's needs in mind. He saw the problem from their point of view. With just over a year in operation, William's business has grown rapidly. He now offers customers his own branded cylinders. He has a team of employees, a warehouse and 4,000 customers. He has a multi-six-figure turnover and is planning for his next product launch in 2022.

The biggest reason for William's exponential growth is his customer-centricity. Knowing his customers well and being able to make decisions that focus on his customer's needs keeps him ahead in the game. At one of William's initial business coaching sessions with me, I asked him what he loves about his business. His answer reveals the secret to his business success. He said, "I love talking to my customers and seeing the smile on their face when I deliver to them." His approach reminds me of Henry Ford, the American industrialist, business magnate and the founder of Ford Motor Company. Ford said, "If there is any one secret of success, it lies in the ability to get the other person's point of view and see things from that person's angle as well as from your own." That is the very essence of William's business. That is also the very essence of this chapter.

> **Honing your ability to see things from your customer's view, as well as your own, is the one skill that will make you and your business stand out.**

In the last few chapters, the focus has been you and your lens on the customer's problems. But your customer may have a very different view of their problems. So, before you start building out solutions to your customer's problems, do some due diligence. Talk to your customers. It is the best way to discover if you have an idea worth pursuing.

Talking to your customer might seem like common sense. But remember the top mistake that founders make from Chapter One. They build things that nobody wants. Why? Because they don't take the time to know more about their customers or even talk to them. At this stage, talking to your customers is not about asking them what solution they want. If they knew the answer to that question, they would've solved it. Nor is it about showingoff your awesome idea. The sole purpose of these conversations is to explore the problem through your customer's lens. Take time to go deep into your customer's mind. Uncover their needs with empathy. This will give you the best chance of building a successful business — a business your customers value. This process, in startup jargon, is called 'customer discovery'.

One of the biggest reasons you must do customer discovery is to gain a competitive advantage and uncover customer insights. By talking to your customers, you will uncover how you can differentiate your solution in the market from their lens. It is the next step in your research as you continue to establish your unique value proposition. In their 2015 research paper, the global consulting firm McKinsey & Company suggests that the ability to capture and use customer insights is critical to the customer's buying experience. Data must be seen as a strategic advantage. They found that when organisations leverage customer behavioural insights, they outperform their peers by 25% in gross margin and 85% in sales growth.

In this chapter, you will learn how to talk to your customers and conduct customer discovery, so that you can unlock customer insights in the next chapter. Unlocking customer insights means you will build something your customers value and want. It is the process of making sure that what you build is fit for purpose and addresses their problems. It increases your chance of success because it lets you get into the mindset and habit of co-creating your business with your customer. It allows you to create solutions that fit your customer's problems. In startup land, it's called creating a 'Problem-Solution' Fit. (You will see more about this in Chapter Ten.) Customer insights also help you understand where to position your products and services in the customer life cycle to increase visibility and sales. (You'll explore more about positioning in Chapter Eight.)

In 2019, when I started my master's degree in entrepreneurship, the whole cohort, 30 of us, were given a challenge on day one. We were asked to build a team with complete strangers and execute a business idea within a week. We had five days to do it all: form a team, come up with an idea, create a business model, build a solution, find paying customers and pitch to a panel of investors. It was startup 101 on steroids.

Without any formal training or frameworks, we just did what we thought was best. The business idea my team decided on was to utilise empty wall spaces in Melbourne for creative and non-invasive light projection advertising. Imagine stepping out of a building and seeing a light projection of Spider-Man swinging along the walls in front of you. What a great way to advertise a Spider-Man movie!

Now imagine if businesses with smaller advertising budgets could afford this for their products and services. A small Vietnamese restaurant around the corner tempting you with a steamy hot *pho* soup on a cold winter evening, or a local clothing store announcing its new line of handmade jackets. This creative way of advertising could be a game-changer for small businesses. Along with small businesses, our target customers were other advertising agencies that didn't have this capability.

We spent the next few days conducting interviews with small-business owners and advertising agencies. Only two out of the many small-business owners that we spoke to were excited about the idea. All the others were sceptical. They wanted to target their local communities more than the people in the city. Since our idea was to use wall spaces of tall buildings which are only in the city precinct, it didn't help the businesses in attracting local customers. The seven advertising agencies that we spoke to had no interest. They said it would never work. They called it 'guerrilla marketing' — a tactic that is seen as irregular and sometimes reputation-damaging for bigger brands, so they didn't want to be associated with us. These interviews gave us a reality check. While we thought it was a great solution for small businesses, we had no clue how they felt about it until we had these conversations.

The other mistake that we made was going in idea-first. We went in with an intention to wow them with this idea because we loved the idea. We didn't go with the intention of discovering more about the problem. We were just shoving an idea down their throats, and who would want that? We had no clue about how to build value in our business idea, nor did we know how to uncover real customer needs. It was our first week learning about the hard truths of entrepreneurship by failing in front of our customers. But it helped us see how crucial the customer input was in building a business. If we hadn't talked to them, we would have spent too much time and money trying to build something that our customers didn't care about. We would have added to that failure statistic from Chapter One. We didn't go ahead with the business idea but scored well on our reflective thesis for the project.

Since then, I have done customer discovery so many times and each time, I learn a better way of doing it. In this chapter, I will show you the simplest way to uncover your customer's needs before you build your solution.

- You will use the customer persona exercise from the previous chapter.

- You will learn where to find people who match your persona, how to talk to them and how to see things from their viewpoint.

- You will understand how to use concepts like design thinking and customer development theories to understand your customers in depth.

And the most exciting part of this chapter is that you will start to find your ideal customers who will be willing to buy from you soon.

Find the right watering holes

There is a common sight every tourist sees on a safari in the African plains and savannas. The sight of animals and birds of different species flocked together at the watering hole, hanging out and quenching their thirst. Take a closer look and you will find that none of the species are there alone. They are always in groups of their own. Human beings have a very similar tendency of hanging out in common places together, either physically or online. People with similar characteristics, preferences and interests are often found in similar places. I call these places 'watering holes'.

In the customer discovery process, your first step is to find your ideal customers so that you can talk to them. Not just the one person that you have described in your customer persona in the previous chapter, but many people who are like your persona. The best place to find them is at their watering hole.

Let me explain this with a little case study. Ram is a change-management consultant from Sydney. He spent a large part of his career working for global corporate firms. About ten years ago, in his 40s, he started his own change-management consulting business. His forte lies in building relationships and, before the pandemic, all his business was through word of mouth and referrals. However, in 2020, he found himself at a point where he had to change the way he did business. He now had to start adopting a more proactive approach in finding customers. But since he never had to find customers before, he didn't know where to start.

I helped Ram with his business model redesign. The first step was to identify his ideal customers. In his problem statement, he identified his ideal customers as medium-sized firms in the retail and manufacturing sectors who were about to embark on a large-scale change and transformation project. He operates in a B2B model, where his business services other businesses. However, since all businesses are run by people, the true customers are the decision-makers in the businesses he wanted to serve. The CEOs, the COOs and the change managers. Once he had clarity on this, he could create an ideal customer persona for these profiles and narrow his focus. But how was he going to reach them?

This is where the watering holes exercise helped him. When doing the exercise, there are two main dimensions to consider — time and space.

Your ideal customer's time can be divided into two parts:

1. Professional time — the time they spend at work
2. Personal time — the time they spend outside of work

Your ideal customer's space can also be divided as:

1. Physical space — where people are in-person
2. Digital space — where they spend time online

For example, in Ram's case, CEOs and COOs like hanging out on the golf course or tennis courts, or watching sport in their personal time. In their professional time, they will be at business networking events, in meetings, commuting to work or at their desk. On the personal side, in an online space you would find them browsing videos on YouTube, watching Netflix, working via their phone or tablets, reading e-books or listening to audiobooks. In their professional time online, they are on platforms like LinkedIn or online networking events.

Examining your customer's watering holes this way gives you a good idea of which time and space dimension you can intercept and interact with them. You may not be able to do it in every space they are in, and I would advise not to (otherwise, they may think of you as an annoying pest). But you can find the right time and space to meet them. In Ram's case, he decided to use the professional time and space to reach his ideal customers, like LinkedIn and networking events, both online and offline. In a B2C business (business-to-consumer model), you might choose to meet them in their personal time and space too. It depends on what kind of problem you are solving.

EXERCISE 17: LIST CUSTOMER WATERING HOLES

In this exercise, you will use your ideal customer persona from the last chapter and reflect on where they may hang out most often.

1. Divide your page into quadrants

Divide your page into four sections. Label the sections along the time and space dimensions as shown on the next page. (There's a template for this on the Jumpstart Studio website.)

Watering Holes

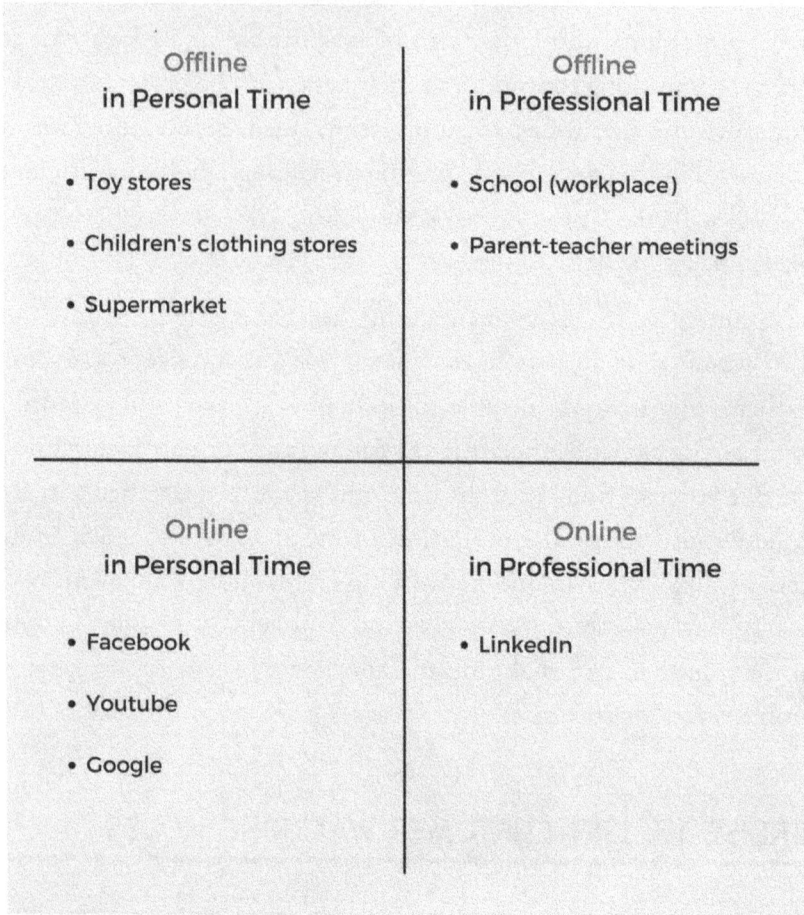

Offline in Personal Time	Offline in Professional Time
• Toy stores • Children's clothing stores • Supermarket	• School (workplace) • Parent-teacher meetings
Online in Personal Time	Online in Professional Time
• Facebook • Youtube • Google	• LinkedIn

2. Populate each quadrant

Make a list of at least five physical and five digital spaces where you will find other people like your ideal customers. In the illustration, I've used Sara from the previous chapter. She's the primary school teacher who needs access to cheaper toys for her seven-year-old son. Some places you would find Sara are toy stores, children's clothing stores, the supermarket and online communities like Facebook Groups and LinkedIn.

3. Choose which to use

Now pick the places where you can meet your customer and start talking to them. Don't feel limited by needing to have in-person conversations. With the pandemic, people have learned how to use online meeting tools in an effective way. Think of innovative ways of having conversations with your ideal customers. At this early stage, you may not want to use all the watering holes you've identified, but you might choose to use them later down the track.

- The purpose of the watering holes exercise is to understand customer's behaviours and preferences in their usual spaces of being. It might sound like the exercise is about stalking them and hunting them down. It's not. The intention here is to find unique ways to reach your ideal customers and have conversations with them.

- You will use these watering holes throughout this book and throughout your business journey. As you get more information about your customers, you can come back and update this list of watering holes.

Get to the root cause

Problems you want to solve for your customer run deeper than you think. At a surface level, you can see the symptoms of a problem. To uncover the true nature and the root cause of a problem and what causes it, you must experience it yourself if possible and have deep conversations with people who experience it.

It's like going to a doctor with a sore throat. A good doctor will want to uncover the root cause of the sore throat, which could be a viral infection, a sinus problem, or a bacterial infection. They do this by asking you questions instead of assuming answers. Depending on the root cause, they prescribe a treatment that is suitable to resolve the problem. However, if the doctor does not evaluate the root cause and offers a solution based on the symptoms or their own assumptions, the real problem will remain unsolved. You will find temporary relief, but the problem-causing infection remains alive in your system, so you continue to remain unwell and suffer. You will lose trust in your doctor's abilities to solve your problem. You will seek help from a different doctor — a competitor, perhaps. This is how you must think of your customer's problems. You want to solve the root cause, not the symptoms.

Solving symptoms causes more harm to your customers and leads to them losing trust in you and your business' ability to solve their real problems. You must solve for the root cause right from the beginning, even before you build your product or service. The risk of not getting to the root cause is wasted time, energy and money in building something that will become obsolete as soon as a competitor uncovers and addresses the root cause.

To uncover the root cause of a problem, you must know what you're going to ask your customers and how. So the next step in this process is to create a customer discovery questionnaire. Set up your questionnaire on a sheet of paper or in an Excel sheet, so that you can record your answers as you have conversations with your customers.

There are two types of questions you must make sure to ask your customers.

1. **Discovery questions** – your aim with these is to discover more about the customer and fill in the gaps in your understanding about their needs and challenges.

2. **Validation questions** – here your aim is to validate your assumptions about the problem, to accept reality, even if it's different from what you think.

Let's look at Sara's example. In her customer persona, I have assumed her goals, challenges, needs and drivers. I have assumed that:

- Her **goal** is to access cheap toys for her son.
- Her **challenge** is the high cost of buying toys for her son and the lack of space and clutter.
- Her **needs** are easy access to toys, the ability to borrow and return whenever she likes, the ability to swap toys often and home delivery.
- Her **drivers** are saving money and space, providing variety in education and entertainment experience for her son, and keeping him occupied.

Interviewing real-life 'Saras' will help me discover more information and validate if my assumptions are right, and ultimately uncover the root cause of her problems.

EXERCISE 18: CREATE YOUR CUSTOMER DISCOVERY QUESTIONNAIRE

One of the best ways to create a customer discovery questionnaire is to use the 'five whys' technique introduced at Toyota in the 1930s. The trick, though, is to interlace the 'why' questions in between your discovery and validation questions. This will make your interview feel more conversational rather than an interrogation. See the example questionnaire you could build for Sara below.

- Tell me a story about the last time you bought toys for your child?
- How was the experience?
- What did you enjoy the most about the experience?
- Why was it so enjoyable?
- What was your biggest challenge?
- Why is it a challenge?
- When it comes to toys for your child, what is the most important thing for you and what is the most important for your child?
- Why do you think that is?
- What bothers you the most?
- Why does it bother you?

Note that all the questions here are open-ended in that they start with what, why, when and how. They are designed to let the customer describe details, and to dive deeper into the details. They do not prompt the customer about your idea or your solution. They're aimed at uncovering the problem at this stage. If your questions are closed-ended — for example, starting with 'do you…?' — they will prompt a yes or no answer from your customer, and you will end up discovering nothing.

How do you know you have reached the root cause during your interviews? Look for emotional responses. When you see the customer's emotions are evoked when answering your questions, you know that you have reached the root cause of the problem.

When they are willing to share details with you that are personal and emotional, that's when you know they really want their problem solved.

Customer interviews can be intimidating if you've never done them before. In the rest of this chapter, I will share with you some of the easiest ways to have these interviews and some best practice tips to make sure you get what you want from them.

Look beyond words

Do you know that in a 30-minute business discussion, two people can send over 800 different non-verbal signals? In her 2012 Forbes article, "Busting 5 Body Language Myths", Carol Gorman, the author of *Stand Out: How to Build Your Leadership Presence*, says that every business interaction has two conversations going at the same time over two channels, verbal and non-verbal. Research shows that 93% of communication can occur non-verbally, revealing underlying emotions, motives and feelings of the person.

As you conduct your customer interviews, remember that people may not always tell you the truth, because they want to look good, seem smart or even impress you. They may also have their own biases towards the problem. So, your job as an entrepreneur who wants to help customers is to get to the root cause of their problems by observing beyond their words.

- Pay attention to the tone of their voice and their body language.

- Watch their behaviour as you ask them the questions.

- Are they at ease?

- Do they make eye contact?

- Are all their answers coherent and in sync?

You are not trying to detect lies here. What you are trying to do is uncover their real behaviours in relation to the problem. For example, if they say the problem is not big or important for them and then fold their arms and look away, it's a clear indication that they are being defensive or have some big challenges with the problem. So, ask the same question again, but in a different way.

Emotional intelligence is as important as conversational intelligence in such situations. One way to capture non-verbal information during your customer interviews is by using the concept of empathy mapping. David and Tom Kelley, founders of IDEO and pioneers in design thinking, introduced the concept of empathy mapping in their *New York Times* bestselling book, *Creative Confidence: Unleashing the Creative Potential Within Us All.* Developed in Stanford University's design department called 'd.school', the empathy map is a tool with four quadrants that allows observational data to be collected in the process of user interviews. The data can then be converted into insights. You will learn more about empathy mapping and insight creation in the next chapter. For now, the following exercise will show you how to make a note of the four key things you must observe when you do your customer interviews.

EXERCISE 19: INCLUDE OBSERVATIONAL QUESTIONS

These questions are for you to answer as you observe the customers during their interviews. In the next chapter, you will use these observations to draw up an empathy map and derive insights.

1. Say

What do people say when you ask them about the problem? What is their tone of voice?

2. Do

What do people do today in relation to the problem? What are they doing when you ask them the questions? What can you infer from their body language?

3. Think

What do people think about the problem? Can they verbalise their thoughts? Can you infer what they are thinking by what they are saying and doing?

4. Feel

How do they feel when you ask them about the problem? Are they able to articulate their feelings? Can you infer their feelings from their words and actions?

Let the conversation flow

Have you met people on the street wanting to survey you for something? One time, as I was walking back home from a long day at work, I was stopped by two people wanting to ask me about my food habits. They told me upfront that they thought many people didn't eat healthy and they wanted to provide a healthy meal service.

Mistake number one was that they told me their version of the problem and the solution upfront. I've seen one too many of those healthy meal services, and even tried a few. In my mind, it already created a bias and a preconceived reference point to their competitors. It influenced the way I responded to the questions.

Mistake number two was that they didn't have a conversation with me. They came with the mindset of a survey, a tick-box exercise to stick with their questionnaire — not with the mindset of uncovering information. They had a long, two-page printed questionnaire that they were trying to complete. As the interview progressed, I got impatient. My answers got shorter. At the end, I refused to give them any personal details like my phone number or email address.

You may have come across such surveys and interviews in the past. The interviewer ploughs through a seemingly never-ending list of questions, making you feel sceptical and that it's a waste of your time. So as you prepare for your own interviews, think about why it made you feel that way and how you could do it in a different way. You want to make your potential customers feel heard and understood, and for them to be willing to talk to you again.

Your questionnaire is a guide to help you uncover answers to the right questions, which is why you have built it before the interview. But don't be too scripted in the way you conduct your interviews. Your aim is to create enough rapport and relatability so that people will give you information you cannot get from just doing an online survey. Ask and listen, observe and capture.

> **Know the questions you want the answers to and then let the conversation flow. Listen more than you speak.**

Knowing how to conduct your customer interviews will lead to insights that can be used as valuable information for your business. Asking questions from a questionnaire and making notes will give you surface-level answers. Your aim should be to reach the emotional layer of the customers to uncover insights.

As you conduct your customer interviews, keep the following seven things in mind:

- Start with easy and rapport-building questions — like asking your customer how their day was or what was the most fun thing they did today.

- Warm up the conversation through active listening. Look at them when they speak and let your body language respond — with a smile or a head nod.

- Respond with paraphrasing what they say back to them to show you understand and care. Clarify anything you may not have understood.

- Ask them questions that you had prepared, but without looking at your notes. Avoid asking leading questions, questions that assume behaviour and action — for example, avoid asking "Do you find buying toys expensive?" Instead, ask, "How does buying toys often make you feel?"

- Ask questions to uncover motivations, feelings and emotions. And where you think they are not giving you deep enough information, ask them to explain further.

- Don't get too friendly, it might jeopardise their answers. So ask your questions and let them take their time to answer.

- Ask for specifics when you don't understand their response and be aware of not influencing your interviewee's answers with your tone of voice and body language. Maintain eye contact but don't interrupt them. Let them finish and wait for a bit of silence before you ask the next question.

There are also some best practice tips you must remember when designing your questionnaire.

1. Design your questionnaire to be a conversation, not an interrogation.

2. Let your customer take centre stage here. No matter how excited you are about your idea, your job at this point is to listen to your customer. So, talk 20% of the time and listen 80% of the time.

3. Don't do this as a tick-box exercise and make a list of 100 questions. Be tactful and ask just enough questions to uncover the root cause of your customer's problems.

4. Do it with respect and if you find a customer doesn't want to talk to you, let them go.

Get out there and do it

Now the most exciting bit of your customer discovery process begins. Talking to your customers!

After all the preparation from the previous chapters and this chapter, you are now ready to get out there and start talking to your potential customers. You know who to talk to, where to find them (you may not want to use all the watering holes, just pick a few for now), what to ask them and how to talk to them. Get out there and start talking to them.

At first, it might seem daunting. The conversations may not flow as you expect them to. And you may feel awkward doing it. But this is what it takes to be a true entrepreneur. Talk to as many people in your ideal target market as you can.

The more you do it, the more comfortable you will get with the process. It will give you insights you will never get from anywhere else.

You are building products that humans will use, so asking a computer what humans need is doing it wrong.

Steve Blank, listed by *Harvard Business Review* as a Master of Innovation and by Forbes as one of the 30 most influential people in 2013, is the author of *The Four Steps to the Epiphany: Successful Strategies for Products that Win* and *The Startup Owner's Manual: The Step-By-Step Guide for Building a Great Company*. He created the four-step customer development method, which in turn led to the lean startup movement in Silicon Valley. Blank suggests that the best way to know if your hypotheses are facts is by getting out of the building and asking people. One of his famous quotes is, "There are no facts inside the building. So get outside."

EXERCISE 20: CONDUCT CUSTOMER INTERVIEWS

1. Set up the interviews

- Set a date and time to do your customer interviews.

- At this stage, aim to conduct at least 25 interviews. There will be more customer interviews and testing to do later.

- Plan for between three to five interviews per day, and pace yourself to give you enough time to process and record the information from the interviews.

- Remember your intention is to understand their problem, not validate your idea.

2. Conduct the interviews

- Use a voice recorder or have a second person taking notes.

- Always ask your customers if you may come back if you need more information.

3. Keep detailed notes

- Use a spreadsheet to record all the information you gather.

- Record names and contact information, along with their responses and your non-verbal observations.

- This will take some time and you might wonder what the point is. This data is going to help you drive the right decisions for your business.

The best part about this exercise is that these 25 customers who were willing to talk to you about their problem are also your potential paying customers. At this point, they are your leads and the list you are creating is a lead list of potential customers. We will explore this concept further in Chapter Nine.

IN SUMMARY . . .

- Businesses are a co-creation. The founder and the customer are on the same team, wanting to solve the same problem. As a founder, you create the solution, but your customer is the one who guides you in discovering the right solution. Your business is here to serve your customers. What better way to lay the foundations than to build the business with your customers along the way?

- You have now learned how to uncover the needs of your customer in a simple and empathetic manner to get to the root cause of the problem. This is not as easy as it sounds, but using the techniques from this chapter, you will be able to step into your customer's shoes and understand their motivations and challenges. Now it's time to get out there and start talking to them. Start gathering as much data as you can.

- Once you have gathered this information from your customers, we will be going back to the drawing board to make sense of it all. In the next chapter, I will show you how to use the information you have gathered and use it to create insights, which will help you formalise the solution you choose to build.

RESOURCES

You can download the Watering Holes template from this chapter on my website www.jumpstartstudio.com.au

Chapter Six

Unlock Insights

In 2021, Melbourne bagged the title for the longest lockdown city in the world. A total of 262 days of lockdown saw many businesses shut down for good. People got used to working from home. The streets in the city were empty and lifeless. During this time, four young professionals decided to change the way Melbournians experienced their city post lockdown. They had a common passion — online gaming. So, they wondered if they could use gamification to help businesses in the city attract more foot traffic. Team Wadoo, short for 'what to do', pitched their idea to the City of Melbourne council and won their support to explore the idea and develop the gamified app. As I began coaching them, the first evident step was to talk to customers. Within one week, they followed all the steps outlined in the last chapter and gathered information from over 30 people in their target market — professionals and students who work in the city. But now what?

Most people think data and information will help them make faster decisions. Many large organisations have decades worth of customer data in their systems — spreadsheet after spreadsheet of customer information. But the truth is that no amount of data and information is of use unless you can convert it into meaningful insights. While large companies have the luxury of hiring data scientists to help them extract meaningful insights, as a startup founder, you will have to do this job yourself.

In this chapter, you will learn how to convert information from your customer interviews into insights. I will show you techniques and tools that you can use over and over throughout your business journey. You will understand how to use these insights to drive business decisions.

Back to the drawing board

Once Team Wadoo had gathered all their customer information, they went back to the drawing board. It was time for them to start converting their data into insights. The process is not as simple as just listing out all the information gathered. Neither is it too complex to warrant using sophisticated data mining tools that large companies use.

> **Converting your data into insights is about looking for patterns in the conversations you have had with your customers and connecting the dots.**

If you don't, all your effort from interviewing the customers is wasted. It becomes a missed opportunity for you and your business.

Atlassian, one of Australia's top software companies, develops workflow and project management products like Jira, Confluence and Trello for businesses. Founded in 2002 with a $10,000 credit card debt, Atlassian listed on the NASDAQ stock exchange in 2015 as a multi-billion-dollar business. To work with customers and understand their needs, Atlassian uses empathy mapping, which I mentioned in the last chapter. They say that creating empathy maps helps them step inside the heads of other people. It helps them identify things like:

- what motivates their customers
- what influences them
- what they need from their product or service.

It helps them derive insights from their user research and foster greater awareness and empathy for their target customers. They also use empathy maps as visual aids on a wall to review and update as they learn more about their customers.

Empathy mapping is used by companies both large and small. Identifying and keeping up with customer behavioural changes and deriving insights is a continuous process that successful companies have adopted. They do this to stay in lockstep with their customers, to understand their needs and improve customer experience. Embedding this behaviour early in your entrepreneurial journey will help you set customer-centricity as a culture within your business too.

In this next exercise, you will use all the information from your customer interviews to create an empathy map. Remember the four things I asked you to observe in the last chapter, as you conducted your interviews — say, do, think, feel? You will now use those observations and the data you have gathered from your interviews to create an empathy map.

EXERCISE 21: CREATE AN EMPATHY MAP

1. Set up your map

- On a whiteboard or a large sheet of paper, draw a four-quadrant empathy map as shown on the next page.
- Name the quadrants 'Say', 'Do', 'Think' and 'Feel'.

2. Allocate interview responses

- As you go through the data you have collected in your interviews, classify each response under one of the quadrants. Use sticky notes to jot down responses one by one and stick the notes in the respective quadrants on your empathy map.
- The purpose of this exercise is to identify patterns from all the data gathered, so make sure you capture both information that the customer told you and information you inferred from your observations.

Here is an example using the interviews from customers like Sara.

Empathy Map

Say	Do

Say

| TOO MUCH CLUTTER IN THE HOUSE | TOYS HARDLY GET USED | KIDS OUTGROW TOYS QUICKLY |
| KIDS PLAY WITH THEIR FAVOURITES MOST TIMES | EXPENSIVE TO KEEP BUYING TOYS | KIDS GET BORED OF THEIR TOYS WITHIN MONTHS |

Do

| THROW AWAY OLD TOYS | PASS THEM ON TO FRIENDS OR FAMILY | GIVE AWAY TO CHARITY |
| SWAP TOYS WITH OTHER PARENTS | ONLY BUY TOYS ON SALE | |

Think

| KIDS HAVE EMOTIONAL CONNECT WITH SOME TOYS | THERE MUST BE A BETTER WAY TO FIND CHEAP TOYS |
| HOW CAN I SAVE MONEY ON BUYING TOYS? | SHOULD BE ABLE TO KEEP SOME TOYS AS MEMORIES |

Feel

| FEAR OF LETTING GO OF THEIR KID'S CHILDHOOD | TIRED AND EXHAUSTED |
| FRUSTRATED | HELPLESS |

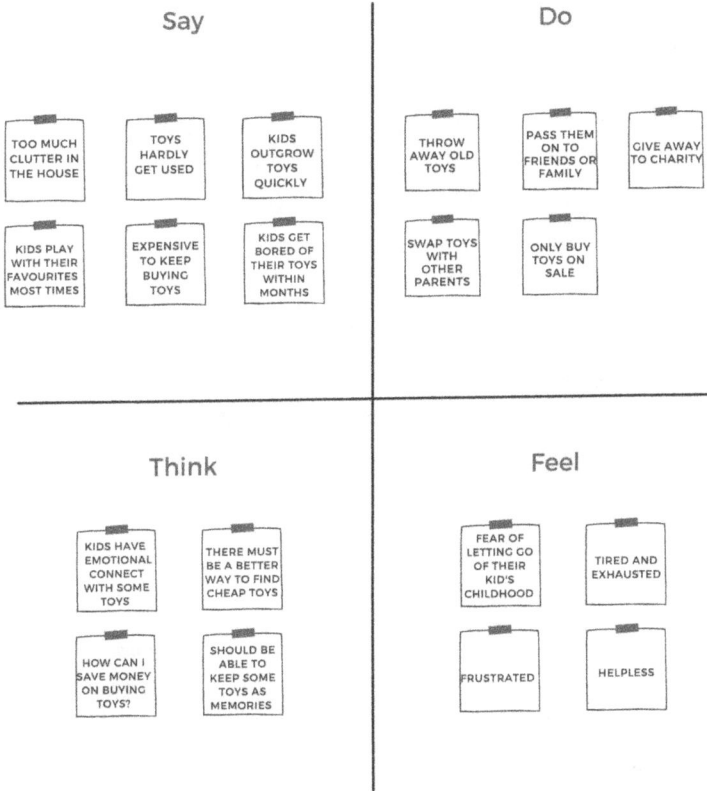

- Once you have mapped out all the responses, you will see some commonalities. There will be some repetition in information from different people. You will also see some outliers.

- Some of the information will validate your current thinking about the problem. There may also be other information that is new and different from the direction you are thinking in.

- The example above validates the problem statement from Chapter Four, where the assumption made was that parents find it expensive to buy toys, children outgrow them and they struggle to find cheap toys. It also introduces new information such as the fear of losing childhood memories. New information is a good sign. This can help you create deeper and more meaningful insights, which in turn will help you build the right solutions.

Dig deeper

Team Wadoo found some incredible insights from their empathy mapping exercise. Through the patterns they saw from their interview responses, they found that not all professionals and students plan activities or things to do. Some people are planners who take the initiative and seek out new and exciting things to do while most of the others just follow them and tag along. They also found that most of the planners used social media platforms like Facebook, Instagram and Google reviews to decide on the events and activities they wanted to attend, and then informed their friends about it. These insights would not have been possible if Team Wadoo didn't take the time to understand the responses from their customers and dig deeper into the empathy map.

Finding insights is a result of identifying patterns. Digging deeper into the patterns can help you find things you never knew existed. It may not seem easy to do at first, but the more you do it you will develop a knack for it. The best insights you can find are emotional insights. Emotions drive people's behaviour. Emotional drivers are the strongest reason why people do things.

> **Understanding your customer's emotional drivers lets you build products that speak to their inner desires. They will relate to your products and services quicker and take action, instead of procrastinating and wondering if they need what you're selling them.**

In 2019, I worked on a project that aimed to solve food waste in households. Australian households throw away 2.5 million tonnes of edible food each year. According to Food Bank Australia, which is a not-for-profit food relief organisation, the average food waste per person equates to 300 kilograms per year. That is one in five shopping bags in every Australian household. In 2019, 690 million people worldwide were affected by hunger, while 45% of the world's fruit and vegetables went to waste. There is enough food on the planet for every single person, yet one in nine people go to bed hungry every night.

So, to understand why people waste food and what their household behaviour patterns are like, my team and I conducted interviews with 12 people. Everyone that we spoke to said that they hated food waste. As we came back to the drawing board and mapped out all the information we had on an empathy map, it was clear that their behaviour didn't reflect their sentiment. Beyond their behaviours and beyond what we observed them say and do, we found that our customers had an emotional connection to food. Over 60% had seen someone in their family struggle to afford food, and 50% had struggled to afford food in the past. So, their sentiment about food waste came from there. Their behaviours however didn't reflect this: 90% of the people we interviewed admitted to wasting food often. This was driven by their current lifestyle. Some of the behaviours we uncovered were lack of time and energy, overspending at the supermarket and being unorganised while shopping. As we connected the dots, it was clear that if our solution was aimed at their emotional drivers, we had a better chance of helping them change their behaviours. After several steps of digging deeper, looking at the food waste lifecycles and working through different business-building steps (which you will also learn about in the coming chapters), we built something simple for our initial solution: a reusable fabric shopping bag with emotional and thought-provoking words and images that would remind people to shop less.

EXERCISE 22: SPOT PATTERNS

To help uncover the deeper meaning of the responses, you can use two techniques: the 'five whys' technique from Toyota that you learned in the previous chapter and the 'what-if' technique from Chapter Two.

1. Look for patterns

To dig deeper into your customer's emotions, look at the think and feel quadrants in your empathy map. Do you see a pattern? Are there any common things that drive people's behaviours?

2. Ask why

To dig deeper into your customer's emotions, ask four or five why questions for each of the common patterns you see until you get to the root cause.

A pattern from the empathy map example is that parents are afraid their children would lose their childhood memories if they gave away all their toys. Use the five whys technique to dig deeper into that emotion.

- Why might that be? Because they will have nothing to hold on to as they grow up.

- Why is that important? Our memories are a big part of who we are and how we develop and shape our personalities.

- Why is that so? Because we're emotional beings and attach an emotional sense to objects.

- Why do we attach emotions to an object? Because it reminds us of who we are and where we come from.

3. Ask 'what if'

Once you have reached the root cause, ask 'what if' to consolidate your thinking.

With the example we can ask, "What if we could help parents access or rent toys at a cheaper price and also have the option to hold on to them?" Now, here's a thought that changes the final solution you will build. It takes into consideration the practical aspects of your solution and the emotional drivers too. We'll dive into this more in the next exercise.

Worst possible idea

Have you ever sat in a meeting and just as someone asks you a question, your mind blanks out? You want to come up with a creative solution to a problem, but the harder you try, the more you can't? It happens to me all the time.

When faced with a problem, people tend to want to find the best idea possible to solve the problem. However, the pressure of having to come up with the best idea kills the creative process. This is where the design thinking technique called 'Worst Possible Idea' comes in handy. It is a great way to shift your thinking and look at things in an unusual way. It gives you creative freedom, which helps you come up with unique solutions for your customer's problems.

The method is about brainstorming multiple ideas to the problem without worrying about the quality of the ideas. Instead of aiming for the best ideas, come up with the worst ideas possible. Generate ideas that you know will fail and don't make any sense. And once you have a whole heap of these, flip them on their head to see if you can find some spectacular ideas. At first, this might seem counterintuitive, but you're doing this to change the direction of your thinking.

The Worst Possible Idea method is noted by the Interaction Design Foundation, the largest online design school, as the method to come up with the silliest, craziest ideas. In their article about the method, they state that, "When design team members identify a rotten-looking or 'preposterous' idea and deconstruct it to see what makes it tick as such, they can find powerful insights that may serve as foundations for good plans elsewhere."

EXERCISE 23: BRAINSTORM SOLUTIONS

This is a fun exercise because you get to dream up terrible solutions, then leverage them into great ones.

The steps are:

1. Look at the 'what if" question (or questions) you've generated.
2. Write down the worst possible ideas you can think of to solve the question.
3. Flip those ideas on their heads.
4. Mix and match the ideas.
5. Rank the ideas to find your best solution.

Let's work this through for our mums looking for cheap toys.

1. Look at the 'what if' question

"What if we could help parents access or rent toys at a cheaper price and also have the option to hold on to them?"

2. Write down all the worst possible ideas you can think of to solve this question

Some worst possible ideas would be:

- Parents must buy all the toys they access with us.
- Our toys will never be for sale.
- Parents are not allowed to keep the toys for more than 30 days or access them ever again.
- Kids may never touch the toys in the toy library.

These ideas don't make sense or even answer the question. They are silly and that's the whole point of this exercise.

3. Flip these ideas on their head so that they align with the question

- Parents can have a choice to buy one or more toys they access each month.
- All toys in the toy library can be sold at a cheaper rate than retail after six to twelve months of use.

- We can help parents take pictures of their child's favourite toys to keep as memories.

- Kids can have a virtual reality version of their toys available forever in the cloud to access later in life or pass on as legacy to their children.

4. Mix and match some of these

You can keep using the what-if technique to help you do this. For example:

- What if, along with accessing or renting toys at a cheaper rate, parents can have the option to buy four toys per year at half price?

- What if we can offer parents an optional play date every month for all children subscribed to the toy library and offer professional photography with every child's favourite toy as a keepsake memory?

- What if we can convert all our toys into 3D virtual reality objects available forever, and kids can choose which ones they like and put them in a virtual vault or the cloud?

5. Rank the ideas to find your best solution

Now rank this list of ideas based on the value to the customer and the ease of implementation for you as a business. Remember that you can just have one idea at the top. Which one will it be? Or can you make them all work together?

Make changes

Team Wadoo used their insights to make changes to their thought process and their intended business model. From the customer interviews and the insights creation process, they learned that they needed to narrow down their customer segment further to professionals and students who plan events and activities. They also learned about the frustrations that these planners had with people dropping out of activities at the last minute and the overwhelm they felt with so much information on social media platforms and so many events to choose from. So instead of going down the gamification route straight away, Team Wadoo decided to first help their customer segment with functionalities that they needed most. Some of these were customised event suggestions, ability to plan and have commitment from all group members within the app, planning missions for groups and individuals to complete in the city. All the people they interviewed are now part of their growing community of first users. Team Wadoo is co-creating their business with their customers. It is bound to be a success.

EXERCISE 24: REVISIT YOUR BUSINESS MODEL AND VALUE PROPOSITION

The purpose of creating insights from your customer interviews is to be able to change the direction of your thinking by understanding what your customer needs first. Use the insights you have gathered in this chapter to revisit your business model in Chapter Three. Your business model must include your customer's voice to be complete and reflective of their problems. So, go back to your business model to fill in any gaps or update with all the insights you've gathered so far. Does your solution and value proposition change? If yes, what should it be now? Go back to your value proposition exercise from Chapter Four and update it too.

It is best to have an open mind and be ready to challenge your previous thinking with the new information that has come to hand. The mindset and attitude you carry while doing this exercise will have a great influence on the value you derive from it.

> **When you start analysing the data and extracting insights from your customer interviews, it is not just to validate your thinking, it is to invalidate any of your incorrect assumptions.**

So be ready to be wrong. That is the most valuable part of the process — to learn something new, to grow in an area where you thought there is nothing more to know.

IN SUMMARY . . .

- This chapter unlocks the gold from your customers. Learning to do this will change the outcome and the success rate of your business. It is the bridge between you and your customers.

- This process of unlocking customer insights will continue for the rest of your business journey and impacts how well your products and services perform in the market. You have now mastered this by using the techniques in this chapter.

- After all this work, you should have a fair idea of what your solution is for your customer. In the next chapter, you will look at how you can start converting this idea into a real business. You will build the first version of your product or service, which you will use to gain paying customers.

RESOURCES

You can download the Empathy Mapping template from this chapter on my website www.jumpstartstudio.com.au

Chapter Seven

Experiment

In 2004, the world was abuzz with new technological developments. The internet was taking over. While Mark Zuckerberg was busy building Facebook, an employee at Google, Orkut Büyükkökten, started building his own online social network named after himself. Much like Facebook, Orkut was designed to help users meet new and old friends and maintain relationships. Fast forward to 2022, Facebook (now Meta) continues to grow by acquiring other social media platforms like Instagram and WhatsApp. However, Google's Orkut didn't fare the same. It was shut down in 2014. Even though Orkut had garnered over 300 million users, other community platforms like Facebook, YouTube and Blogger had outpaced Orkut in growth.

You may be surprised to know that there is a whole website dedicated to Google's product failures. As of August 2021, killedbygoogle.com, which is developed and maintained by software developer Cody Ogden, lists 232 products that have been abandoned by Google over the years. On Pinterest, the social media platform, there are dedicated pages to failures by large technology companies. Look up the Microsoft Morgue to learn about some interesting products that a giant like Microsoft was unable to save from the clutches of failure.

Failure is a beast that even the largest of companies are unable to dodge. Alberto Savoia, Google's first engineering director and the author of *The Right It: Why So Many Ideas Fail and How to Make Sure Yours Succeed*, describes the law of market failure in his book. He says that most new products will fail in the market even if they are executed well. In his opinion, there exists at least five failures for every success. The key to increasing your odds against failure is to test if the market wants to buy your ideas before you build them. You do this by testing your ideas in the simplest way possible.

You may have heard of the terms 'prototype' and 'minimum viable product' (MVP). A prototype is the first version of your actual solution. A version that your users can touch and feel. For example, to build a leather backpack, you could first prototype it as a paper backpack to test the design and structure. An MVP is the first viable version of your solution, a version that has the basic functionality that your customers can use, and that you can sell. For example, no one will buy a paper backpack, but if you evolved it into a canvas or fabric backpack, you could sell it in the market. This is your MVP, a version of your final product that covers the basic functionality.

In his book, Savoia introduces the concept of a 'pretotype', which was developed by him at Google in 2009. A pretend version of your solution. A version to test if users want your solution before you start building a prototype. He says 'pretotyping' is the process of quickly and cheaply validating if an idea or solution is worth pursuing. The concept is not to test: can we build it? That is done in the next step when you prototype or build an MVP. But rather to test: if we build it, will they buy it? In the backpack example, this means that even before you make a paper version, create some mock designs online and advertise them to see if people are interested in buying.

Phases of Rapid Experimentation & Testing

Both pretotyping and prototyping can be mixed to create rapid experiments for testing your solution in the market. Rapid experimentation prevents

111

you from building the wrong solutions. The purpose is to use the least amount of time and resources to validate your ideas. It is the quickest way to experiment and rule out ideas that won't work.

> **Knowing that your customers will buy what you build, and not having to guess the outcome of your hard work gives you confidence and sets you up for success, even before you've started building your products and services.**

To practise what he preaches, Savoia even pretotyped his own book before he wrote it. He spent five days writing a short booklet on pretotyping concepts and techniques, called *Prototype It: Make Sure You are Building the Right It Before You Build It Right*, printed a few dozen copies, stapled them and handed them out to colleagues and friends. When he started receiving more requests for the booklet, got feedback from people applying the techniques and was invited to give talks and conduct workshops on the subject, he knew it was worth investing the time and effort to write a proper book.

Over the years, I have seen many different teams try out different pretotyping and prototyping methods. However, there are three methods that I have seen work well for 95% of products and services. In this chapter, you will learn these three methods — how to run the experiments, what data to collect and how to assess the outcomes.

Data is king

Remember Foodtropia? My food business from Chapter Three that was about having dinner parties in strangers' homes. After extensive customer interviews and learning that grandmas didn't want to cook for strangers, we changed our business idea. The first step to do that was to test if people even wanted to go to other people's homes to eat in the first place. Our solution was to have a cultural dinner party instead, but we didn't have anything planned. We wanted to test the market to see if people liked the idea before we invested any money in organising the party. Within a few minutes, we came up with the experiment we wanted to do — a traditional Spanish at-home dinner party hosted by my co-founder Dario, who was a renowned hotelier from Spain. We decided on a time and date and kept the exact address and dinner menu secret to create a bit of mystery. We designed and published an advertisement on Facebook and Instagram aimed to attract our target market, which was young professionals who worked in the city. We priced the three-course meal including wine at $50, which was great value for money compared to a restaurant meal. But how would we know if our test was a success or not?

Before you learn the different methods of rapid experimentation, it's important to understand why you are conducting these experiments. Your goal with these experiments is to gather your own data from customers that will allow you to make the right decisions about your business.

> **Data = facts. Working off facts is always going to give you a better chance of success than working off assumptions.**

You could work off other people's data and information but working off data that you have collected for your own products or service is the best way to tell if your solution has value in the market. Just like you did your own customer interviews to understand the problem, you must collect your own data for your solution to see if it fits the problem, to achieve a problem-solution fit.

There are four types of data that your customers can give you:

- attention
- time
- personal information
- money.

Each of these data types holds a certain level of value. Validation for your solution occurs when customers are willing to exchange their data to get your solution. It is this transaction that tells you what kind of value your idea holds in the customer's mind. There are three different levels of value attached to your customer's data.

1. Low-value data

When a customer is willing to give you brief time and attention, maybe less than 30 seconds, it's classified as low-value data.

Examples include:

- views or likes on your social media posts
- a brief read of your emails, one-line opinions and comments on social media.

Fake personal information is also classified as low-value data, as the person doesn't want to connect with you. Ever given away a fake email address or a wrong phone number to get something in return? Did you value what you got in return?

2. Medium-value data

When someone goes the next step and is willing to give you personal information or feedback, you know they value your solution. This is classified as medium-value data.

Examples include:

- home address or email address
- personal feedback to improve your product or service
- word of mouth sharing with their own networks
- credit card information for a free trial
- recruiting friends and family to use your product or service
- providing you contacts in their network.

3. High-value data

The best example of a high-value data is money. This is the next step from medium-value data.

Examples include:

- a deposit to secure your product or service
- investing in your product development
- a pre-purchase of your product at full price.

Customer Data Classification

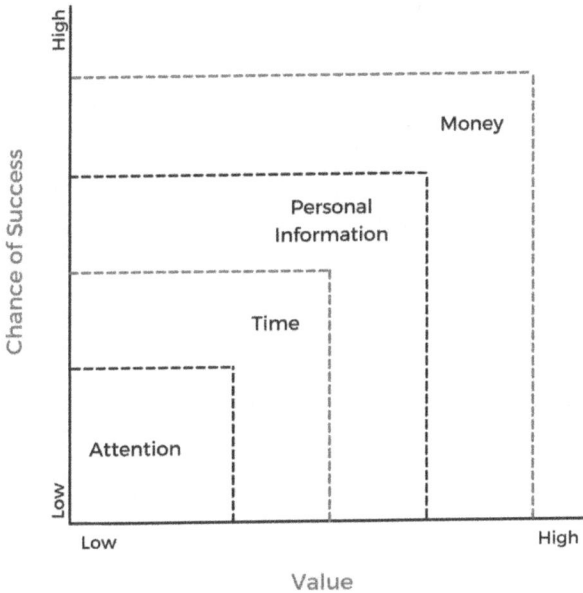

The goal for every business is to gather sufficient high-value data from their customers to ensure a higher chance of success. The two things to consider are quality and quantity.

1. Quality

When someone pays you money, you know you have a business. For Foodtropia, we aimed to get high-value data right from the start. Even with the first experiment, we advertised the dinner at $50 per person. If people didn't pay us the money, we knew our idea didn't have potential. I will show you more about how you can aim to get high-value data right from the start in this chapter and the next few chapters.

You could aim to also collect medium-value data like personal information for a start if you like, but the higher the data in value, the more confident you can be in building your solution.

2. Quantity

In addition to the quality of the data, identify how much data you need from customers to establish if your idea is valuable or not. This is called an 'experimentation threshold'. For Foodtropia, we had six seats available at the dinner party. If we sold four seats (67%), it would cover the costs for the dinner. So that was what we used as a measure of success. We ended up selling five seats at the dinner (83%), paid for upfront. This was enough to tell us our experiment was a success. Now the decision was ours if we wanted to go ahead with the dinner party or not.

Experimentation thresholds

As you go through the rapid experimentation process and use the methods in the rest of this chapter, you will need to identify what data you would like to collect. Here are some good starting examples:

- email addresses
- phone numbers
- money — partial deposit or the full price.

You will then need to identify how many people you want to reach with these methods, and what percentage of those people must give you their data for you to know that your idea is valuable.

Let's say you want to collect real email addresses from interested customers. You test with 1,000 ideal customers. This is a big number but don't worry, I'll show you how to do this here and in the next chapter. You set a threshold of 10%. This means that if 100 people out of those 1,000 people give you their real email address, your experiment is a success. If not, it's time to go back to the drawing board and work on your solution. Or pick your second-best solution (if you have one).

If you have achieved your threshold or more, then it is a clear indication that your solution has desirability in the market and you can move forward with your idea.

Rapid experiment method one: landing page

In late 2012, four students at Stanford University were looking for a startup idea to help local businesses. They set out to interview local businesses to understand their pain points and challenges. As they were wrapping up an interview in a macaroon shop in Palo Alto, they overheard the manager turn down a delivery order from a customer. This was their light-bulb moment. They wondered, 'What if businesses could send things across town on demand?' Most restaurants didn't deliver and those that did told them that delivery was their biggest frustration. The four students decided to run an experiment to test their idea in the market. That afternoon, they put together a landing page — a one-page website that laid out basic information about their business. They found a few menus of restaurants in Palo Alto, stuck them on their landing page and added a phone number at the bottom — which was their own personal phone number. And that was it. They called it paloaltodelivery.com. They weren't expecting anything. All they wanted to see was if anyone would call. And if they got enough phone calls, then maybe this delivery idea was worth pursuing.

All of a sudden, they got a phone call. Someone placed an order for Thai food delivery. They didn't know what to do. But because they were free at that time, they picked up the food and delivered it themselves. In the process, they got an opportunity to talk to a real customer. The next day, they got two more phone calls. The day after, they got five, and the day after that, they got seven. Soon, paloaltodelivery.com started becoming well-known across the campus. A simple landing page is how America's biggest online food delivery service, DoorDash, was born. Today DoorDash commands 56% market share and is bigger than its closest rival UberEATS.

In today's environment, a landing page is a must for every business. Whether you are a product business or a service business, whether you intend to have a physical brick-and-mortar store or an online store, a landing page is the easiest way for you to establish presence and conduct experiments. It creates legitimacy for your business. With a big shift to online during the COVID-19 pandemic, people want to see a website to know that you are a real business.

The aim of your landing page is to showcase one single product and service, and not distract your customers with multiple offers. Your customers will land on this page to learn more about your product or service. The page must capture data from your customers — medium to high-value data.

Many people think they need to hire a professional to build a landing page. Maybe you do. But if your computer skills are reasonable, anyone can build a landing page today. At this stage of the process where you are experimenting, don't spend too much money. You might have to end up making a few different landing pages to test different ideas, based on your results. So be careful with how much you spend.

EXERCISE 25: BUILD A LANDING PAGE

There are many tools available today to help you build no-code landing pages. That means you don't need to be a software developer or a designer to build professional-looking landing pages. These tools have ready templates available for you to use. If you are still unsure, get someone in your network like a family member or a friend to help you. Or look for a freelancer on upwork.com or fiverr.com. Even if someone else helps you now or later down the track, remember this is your business, so you must know the basics of how to do this and how it all works. So give it a go.

1. Find the right provider

Some landing page providers that I recommend are:

- Wix.com – Cheap and easy to use templates with reasonable designs

- Squarespace.com – Great designs, although a bit more expensive than wix.com

- Burnerpage.com – Pre-modelled basic landing pages that take a few minutes to customise

- Unbounce.com – Landing pages with more built-in analytics.

2. Write the content from the customer perspective

For the content, make use of all the customer information and insights you have collected in your interviews from the last two chapters. Word it from a customer's perspective, not just your own. Use the words they used when you interviewed them. In our example of Sara and customers like her, did they say the words 'clutter' or 'mess'? Was Sara's challenge 'buying expensive toys' or 'finding cheap toys'? It's these little nuances that will help your message resonate with people who land on your page.

Make sure your page highlights the following key points:

- the problem and value proposition for your product and service to the customer

- key outcomes for the customer

- the specific benefits they can expect when using your product or service

- features for your product or service

- the estimated price

- a call to action.

3. Decide your call to action

A call to action is where you will prompt the customer to leave their data for you — such as an email, a phone number, or a dollar deposit. The call to action can be placed in multiple places on the page. Experts suggest having at least three to five calls to action throughout the page. You may wonder what your customer gets in return for leaving their data. I'll tell you more in Chapter Nine.

4. Test and check

Before you go live, test your page to make sure all the links are correct. I'd also recommend sending it to a friend to test how easy and clear it is to navigate. Also ask them to check for any typos or mistakes — you will have read your content so often that you won't be able to see them.

5. Go live

Don't worry if your landing page is not perfect. Remember, the initial DoorDash landing page was made in an afternoon and it was very basic, yet it worked. As long as you include the information I have outlined for you here, you are good to go. At the beginning of your journey, speed is more important than perfection. So, hack things together until you get some data and validation to make your decisions.

Rapid experiment method two: explainer videos

The easiest way to double your sales is to show customers a video of your solution. Research by CrowdRiff, a Canadian visual marketing company, found that using a video on your landing page can increase purchases by 86%. They say that visual decision-making is an exploding trend. Brands must leverage visual content in their marketing to capitalise on this behaviour.

In this second experimentation method, you will learn how to create videos that explain your solution in an interesting way to your customers — even before you build anything. An explainer video allows your customers to see what your product or service can do for them.

The advantage of using videos is that they appeal to two of the most important human senses: sight and sound. This helps people understand and retain information for longer. Videos make your idea more compelling and real than just the written word. However, videos do take longer to make, and they need a strong storytelling ability.

Explainer videos can be of two types:

- Animation videos: these videos explain your solution using animated storytelling. They are excellent for both product and service type solutions.

- Show-and-tell videos: in these videos, your product or service is explained by you. Much like the show-and-tell events at children's schools, these videos are best done using some props, like a mock-up of your product using paper or 3D printing, a few slides on Microsoft PowerPoint, or on a whiteboard to draw and describe your product or service.

Some good examples for explainer videos can be seen on YouTube. Look up Fond, which is an employee engagement business. They have a great animated explainer video. Certainly.io, an e-commerce platform, also has a catchy animated explainer video on YouTube. For a landing page with an explainer video, look at upzeez.com which showcases a vertical moving mobile baby cot to help parents avoid back pain.

EXERCISE 26: MAKE AN EXPLAINER VIDEO

Like the landing page method, at this stage you only need a basic explainer video, which is about one to two minutes long.

1. Work out the story

Your video must tell a story. Here is a high-level story structure that works well for an explainer video.

- Start by portraying your ideal customer, showing the problem they face and how it makes them feel. Think of Sara from the toy library example.

- Introduce your solution and show the customer using the solution — the toy library and the features you intend to provide Sara, such as easy access to use toys, low subscription rates and home delivery.

- Now show how the solution benefits your customer, how it makes them feel and why they love it. Call out any additional features, such as the ability to buy toys at half price, for example.

- End with a call to action, like directing your customers to a landing page or asking them to email or call a specific number. Just one action.

2. Decide the key action

The purpose of the video is to collect medium to high-value customer data. Think of the key action they need to do to give you the data. Maybe click a link at the end or send you an email to a specific email address.

3. Make or commission the video

You can do the videos yourself or get professional help. For the show-and-tell videos, all you need is a phone with a good camera, a little stand to hold your phone, and a basic video editing software that lets you cut out bits and add some sound. For the animation videos, you could use templates from websites like:

- Vimeo.com – Excellent guided templates to help you build professional-looking videos

- Doodly.com – To create professional doodle videos

- Moovly.com – To create animated and presentation style videos

If you decide to get professional help with creating videos, hire digital video freelancers from websites like upwork.com and fiverr.com. Although this is a more expensive option than doing it yourself, it is worth it if you struggle with creative design and are willing to spend a little bit of money to save time.

4. Put it out there

Once you've made it, you could use the video:

- on your landing page to double the impact

- on popular social media platforms like YouTube
- to show to your customers in-person
- for advertising (which we will discuss more in the next chapter).

Rapid experiment method three: overlay

I must warn you about this method. It is not everyone's cup of tea. But it is one of the most rewarding experimentation methods if you set it up and execute it well.

The overlay experimentation method is an excellent testing method for physical product ideas. It straddles the line between pretotyping and prototyping. It's where you take an existing product that looks and feels like the product you intend to build, then overlay it with additional features you intend your product to have. Remember, your intent is not to sell this pretotype, but to gather data from customers.

The overlay method lets you gather more robust and qualitative data than the above two methods. Your customers can touch and feel your product and give you direct feedback in person. It gives you the confidence that once you manufacture your product, people will buy it.

EXERCISE 27: CREATE YOUR OVERLAY EXPERIMENT

Let's say your new product idea is potato chips dipped in Belgian chocolate. You intend to pack it in long cylindrical boxes. To test if your target customers will buy your chips, create a label with a clear logo and a description saying, 'chocolate-dipped baked potato chips.' If you can, put a picture on the label to show what the chips will look like. Use canva.com to design your labels. It's easy and free to use. You could hire freelancers on upwork.com or fiverr.com if you like as well.

Now buy a few cylindrical boxes of the size and shape you want them to be. Fill them with chips from any other brand. Overlay the box with your label and branding. For all purposes, it should look and feel like your unique product. Your intention is to show this product to your customers and gather data on whether they would buy it. Remember, we don't want to do a survey here; it's about observing natural customer behaviour. So don't stand on the streets and ask people if they want to buy your chips.

We will talk more about market positioning in the next chapter. But to show you how this experiment method works, place your overlaid sample chips in a location you intend to sell your real product — for example, on a supermarket shelf — and observe if people take your product to the checkout counters. Of course, you will need to get permission for this. You might find more luck with smaller grocery stores or local market stores than large supermarket chains. When you see people picking up your product and wanting to pay for it, that's when you know your idea has legs. It gives you solid data on how many people would or would not buy it if your product was on the shelf.

Remember, you're not selling the product at this stage. You must intervene with the customer before the purchase takes place. So, when a customer picks up your box of chips and puts it in their basket — that is a good enough sign they will buy it. At this point, approach the customer, tell them it's an experiment. Take this opportunity to do a bit of customer discovery. Strike up a conversation and ask them why they picked up your chips compared to the others? What did they like about it? Then ask if you can contact them when the real product is ready. Thank them for their time and give them a free bag of chocolates or chips. This will give you some qualitative data. And because data is king, even though they haven't paid money for it, for the purposes of your experiment — you can count this as high-value data. They would have paid for it if you didn't intervene. Now set a threshold for this experiment as you would with the previous methods — for example, if 20% of people in the chips aisle put your product in their basket, you have a winner.

You may wonder if this is legal to do. You may also wonder what people will think about you for doing this. However, remember that you are experimenting here. You don't intend to collect money from the customers in this method. Your product is not even registered on the supermarket or grocery store's system. Your sole purpose is to collect customer feedback and data.

IN SUMMARY . . .

- When you have a brand-new idea and don't know if the market wants to pay you for it, rapid experimentation is the best way to go. This chapter teaches you how to do that by showcasing the very first version of your solution — a version to test if people will buy your product or service before you build it.

- Don't be afraid to mix and match some of the methods you have learned in this chapter, or even create a new one if you like. The whole idea is to pretend your product exists — using the least amount of time, effort and money to create it.

- In the next chapter, you will learn how to position your experiments in the market with your customers so that there are hundreds and thousands of people starting to look at your product and service and wanting it.

RESOURCES

You can access a 45-minute Masterclass on my website to learn ten different pretotyping and prototyping methods — www.jumpstartstudio.com.au

Chapter Eight

Position in the Market

Ever attempted public speaking in front of a large audience? There's a feeling you have just before you get on stage to start your speech. Are people going to like it? What will they think about me? How will they react? Are they going to laugh at me? But think about all the work you do before you get to that point. You spend time understanding who your audience is, why they are there to listen to you, and what you can say to them to get your message across.

Launching your ideas and experiments in the market can feel much the same. After all, you are showcasing your thoughts and creativity to the world. Are you excited? Nervous? Wondering what people are going to think about you? Good. This is where you should be. Hang in there for just a little bit longer.

The process of entrepreneurship is all about leaning into your vulnerabilities. You will gather fans along the way. There will also be some naysayers. But know this, there are several people who are being inspired by you too.

> **The courage you show by putting yourself and your thoughts out there will be the biggest growth you will ever experience in your journey. So, feel the nervous excitement and do it anyway.**

Experiments can either fail or succeed. In this chapter, I will show you how you can position your experiments in the market so that you have the best chance of success. The aim is to get the maximum number of people looking at your experiment and giving you their data. So, before you hit the market with your shiny new experiment, let's look at how to position your solution so that you can get the maximum number of people looking at it. How you position your product or service in the market matters just as much as the quality of what you put out in the market. Understanding what your customers' buying behaviours are and where to place your product or service so that it meets the customers' needs will determine the success rate of your experiments.

This chapter will help you reach maximum customers from the get-go. This is the final step of all your hard work from the last seven chapters in this book. It is also the first step to showing the world your idea in a structured and effective way that compels them to act. Meeting the threshold you've set in the previous chapter for your experiment depends on how you use the concepts from this chapter. The fundamental marketing concepts in this chapter will also help you throughout your business journey.

In their book *Positioning: How to be Seen and Heard in the Overcrowded Marketplace*, first published in 2001, renowned marketing strategists Al Ries and Jack Trout emphasise the importance and impact of companies taking a unique position in the market. Over time though, positioning has become a lost art that many people — even marketers — overlook.

In an article called "Why Positioning is More Important than Ever" published in 2020, in the American magazine *Entrepreneur*, Andrea Olsen, a behavioural science-based marketing expert who works with consulting firms like EY and McKinsey, says, "Effective positioning ensures that marketing messages help you stand out, resonate with target consumers and compel them to take action. If you're not standing out, you're not positioning."

This chapter is about positioning your solution in the market to meet the customer where they are. You will learn key positioning strategies such as:

- marketing funnels

- customer journey mapping
- push-pull factors.

You will then use these strategies to create your marketing messages and learn how to make them visible to your audience.

AIDA marketing funnel

The Super Bowl is one of America's biggest sporting events. It is the annual championship game of the National Football League, played in February every year. In 2018, pop music megastar Justin Timberlake performed at the Super Bowl during half-time. Within minutes after the show, Nike sold out their $200 limited edition Air Jordan III 'JTH' shoes as soon as they launched. You guessed it right, Timberlake was wearing the shoes.

Most people think that when celebrities endorse products, they sell like hot cakes. The reality is that there is a structured process that sits behind the scenes, which drives customer behaviour. The endorsement is the tip of the iceberg. Elias St. Elmo Lewis, an advertising expert from the 19th century and author of books like *Financial Advertising* and *Getting the Most out of Business*, established a marketing model called AIDA. It is a classic marketing model used today, even after 120 years, by businesses both big and small.

AIDA model is one of the simplest marketing models you can use at this stage of your business. It works for all kinds of businesses. AIDA is short for the four stages in the model:

1. Awareness – This is the first stage where people become aware of your product or service for the first time. You must aim to get the maximum number of people within your target market to become aware.

2. Interest – A subsection of people who are aware of your product will start showing interest. In marketing and sales speak, these

people are called 'leads' — people showing a higher indication of purchase than others.

3. Desire – At this stage, some of your leads will start to desire your product or service. They are called 'prospects'.

4. Action – This is where the final purchase of your solution will take place and some of your prospects will become your paying customers.

Before the Nike Air Jordan shoes sold out in 2018, the company implemented the AIDA model to create awareness, build interest and establish desire for the product in the market. Craig Huey, an award-winning marketing guru, evaluates Nike's AIDA model in his blog titled "How Nike Used the Super Bowl to Create Buzz and Dramatically Boost Sales". This is how it played out.

- Awareness – Nike kicked off the awareness process by posting about the limited edition shoes on their SNKRS app a few days before the Super Bowl. They showcased the design of the shoe, which was not yet available on the market.

- Interest – Viewers who use Nike's SNKRS app were shown pictures of the shoes over and over again to pique their interest.

- Desire – Before the show, Timberlake posted a photo on Instagram to highlight the shoes he was wearing. The post received more than 2.6 million likes and started creating desire.

- Action – As soon as Timberlake's performance finished, tens of thousands of Nike SNKRS app users received a notification on their phones calling them to purchase the shoe on a special landing page. Nike made the purchasing process as simple as possible for its customers. The exclusivity of the product added fuel to the fire.

This entire marketing strategy generated $2.68 million for Nike and was a huge success.

AIDA Marketing Funnel

Awareness

Interest

Desire

Action

The AIDA model is also called a 'marketing funnel'. At every stage of the model, customers are distilled into the next stage. This means that not everyone who enters the awareness stage of the AIDA model for your solution will end up buying it. At every stage, a small percentage of customers will trickle down to the next stage. So the more people are aware of your product or service, the more they will flow through the next stages of the funnel. There is no benchmark to what percentage of customers move between each stage. It depends on your solution, the industry and the marketing activities you conduct at each stage.

EXERCISE 28: DEVELOP YOUR MARKETING FUNNEL

Your aim at this point is to think about all the different ways you can create maximum awareness about your solution. You've already done half the work in Chapter Five by identifying watering holes and where to find your customers. Now it's time to design your marketing funnel and identify the steps you must take to reach your customers.

1. Work out your MVP

Before you start, if you haven't figured out how to deliver your product or service to your customer yet, work that out first. You don't need the final version of your solution, but you do need to know how you can give them a functioning solution, an MVP, that will deliver all that you have promised the customer. More about delivery in Chapter Nine.

2. Design your funnel

Let's look at this using our toy library example. Imagine you have created a landing page with a two-minute video explainer for the toy library. You could design the marketing funnel in this manner:

Awareness

List the places you will find most of your target market. Think online and physical watering holes such as Facebook groups and toy stores. Consider how you will make your customers aware of your toy library: Facebook posts and ads, Google ads, Google listing, word of mouth from other mums, printed flyers or posters in the right places. All this should lead them to your landing page. I will show you how to create some of these further in this chapter.

Interest

Not everyone who becomes aware of your toy library will be interested. But some will. They will click on your ads or see your information and visit your landing page. If they stay for longer than two to three minutes on your landing page, you know they have watched the video. Track this using the tools that your landing page provider offers. If you need some professional help with this, lean on people with the know-how — family, friends, or a freelancer.

Desire

Some people who land on your page will want to know more. They desire your toy library service. This is when they will give you their medium and high-value data. It's always nice to be able to give them something back in return for this information.

For example, you could offer a downloadable list of ten places to buy the cheapest toys for six to ten-year-olds in exchange for their email address. Such giveaways are called 'lead magnets'. They attract your leads and convert them into prospects. Another example is to offer limited-time one-month trial of your toy library for $10. This way, you are encouraging them to take action straightaway and you are collecting some money.

The likelihood that someone will pay you money the first time they land on your page is very low. However, that doesn't mean you shouldn't have the option for them to do that. You'll learn more about creating irresistible offers in the next chapter.

If you don't intend to deliver your MVP to your customers in the next few months, then don't collect money in your experiments. You can still run the experiment but send any customer who hits the 'buy now' button to a thank you page and offer them something in return. For example, in the toy library scenario, you could thank them for their time with a $5 voucher at their nearest toy store.

Action

Customers are more likely to give you their email address. It's your job to nurture and influence them to make a purchase. To encourage take-up of your $10 pre-launch offer, you could send them a series of follow-up emails. Remember how Nike kept showing pictures of their yet-to-be launched shoe over and over again to their customer. Front of sight is front of mind. So don't shy away from sending your prospects information about your product to keep them interested and desiring. You can set up automated emails using platforms like Mailchimp.com. You don't want to spam them, so make sure your emails are informative and offer great value to your customers.

Customer journey mapping

In business, knowing where and how to reach your customers is not enough. Knowing the right moments in time to reach them can have a big influence on their behaviour. A leading over-the-counter medicine brand found that people who took medication within the first two days of symptoms are more likely to get relief and become brand advocates. With this data at hand, the company worked with Google and WebMD, the largest database for medical advice online, to reach consumers who searched for related symptoms online, within that narrow two-day timeframe. As a result, their searches to sales conversions increased and they built greater brand loyalty at the same time. Partners at the consulting firm Bain & Company, Laura Beaudin and Francine Gierak, talk about the importance of timing in marketing in their article, "It's About Time: Why your Marketing May be Falling Short". In joint research with Google, involving 1,700 marketers, they found that, "By communicating at the most opportune times based on people's behaviour and signals, companies can generate more business with fewer or more efficient ads or expand the audience to find unexpected wins."

Presenting the right solution to a problem at the wrong time is like handing a band-aid to someone who hasn't cut their finger yet. Just because someone knows they may have a problem is not reason enough for them to do something different.

> **If you offer a solution when they're experiencing the problem in real time, that is when your highest chances of success are — not before and not after.**

With the rise of digital channels, marketing and reaching your customers has become easier than ever before. Every other company out there is trying to get ahead in the race. However, how many times have you seen an advertisement on your phone while browsing social media and you've just ignored it? It didn't interest you because you didn't have the problem at that moment in time. Timing plays a big role in positioning your product or service in front of the customer.

A customer journey map is a tool to chart your customer's behaviour and identify the right time to reach them. It outlines your customer's actions related to the problem in a step-by-step process. Mapping this step-by-step process gives you a clear view of where the customer is experiencing most pain with the problem and their current solution. Once you identify the exact time in the journey your customer feels the pain, you can then position awareness activities from your AIDA model. This will get your customer to notice you straight away because you have been strategic about your positioning. You will become visible and available to them at a point in time where it matters most to them.

If you position your AIDA model at the wrong point in time in the customer's journey, you won't be able to attract enough interest in your solution. This has a direct impact on the number of customers you will gain.

EXERCISE 29: CONSTRUCT A CUSTOMER JOURNEY MAP

You have already gathered all the information you need for your customer journey mapping during your customer interviews in Chapter Five. For example, for our toy library scenario, we have spoken to Sara and other people like her and established that her goal is to access cheap toys for her seven-year-old son. We've learned that she uses a Facebook group called, 'Used toys for kids 6 to10 years old'.

Now we can map out her journey in a step-by-step format as shown on the next page. (This template is available on the Jumpstart Studio website for you to do your own.)

1. Map your customer's journey

	Step 1	Step 2	Step 3	Step 4	Step 5	Step 6	Step 7	Step 8	Step 9
Actions	Picks up her phone and opens the Facebook app	Scrolls through her feed and likes a few posts	Goes to the "Used Toys for 6-10 year olds" Group	Scrolls through many posts and toys	Finds one that she likes	Leaves a comment on the post	Scrolls some more and then logs off	Receives a reply, negotiates price and arranges a time for pick up	Drives 20 minutes to pick the toy up
Thinking	This is such a chore, I just want to sleep	Why are people on Facebook all the time?	Let me just find some toys for Ryan quickly and I can go to bed	Will I find any suitable toys for Ryan here?	Oh this looks good!	I hope it's still available	Are there any more, incase that one is sold already?	Finally! But I'll have it during my lunch break tomorrow	I hope the lady is home and the toy is not broken or dirty
Feeling	Tired and disinterested	Amused	Rational	Anxious	Relieved	Hopeful	Nervous	Happy but worried	Stressed
Pain Point	Anticipation of wasted time	Distractions add more time to the process	Unorganised catalogue of items	Wasted effort and no guarantee of finding toys	Can't tell if it is clean and in good condition	No way of knowing if it is available or she will get a reply	Needs to still keep searching	No way of knowing if she is overpaying or the seller is genuine	Travel-time and uncertainty
Desire	There was an easier way to get cheap toys	There was a single place for these used toys	This group had more interesting stuff	There was a way to see which toys will be suitable quickly	I could see more information about the toy	There was a way to see which toys are still available	Didn't have to search so much	Didn't have to negotiate or do this during work hours	Could get the toys delivered instead
Day, Time & Location	Day 1 9pm on the couch	Day 1 9.01pm on the couch	Day 1 9.10pm on the couch	Day 1 9.20pm on the couch	Day 1 9.25pm on the couch	Day 1 9.25pm on the couch	Day 1 9.30pm on the couch	Day 2 11am at work (school)	Day 3 12.30am in the car

2. Identify the right moments to reach them

Once you've mapped out the journey, you can identify the different steps at which she feels the most pain and when in her journey will she take notice of the toy library and want to know more.

Let's do this with the example journey map:

- Looking at the journey map, where could we introduce awareness activities? Focus on the 'feelings' and the 'desire' sections in the map. Where do you think she is feeling the most pain?

- Step 2 to Step 4 in the journey map is where she seems to be experiencing most of the pain around ease of access. So if we place Facebook ads and posts in steps two, three and four, she is bound to take notice, which is raising her awareness.

- At Step 8, her pain point is negotiating with people on Facebook groups. So if we stick up some posters and flyers in her school, where she must negotiate and is thinking about it, we have a higher chance of getting her interested.

This is how Sara will move from the awareness stage to the interest stage on the AIDA model.

The push-pull dynamic

No matter how unique your solution is, your customers are already doing something today to solve their problems. When you present an alternate solution to their problem, the push-pull dynamic will come into play.

> **The push-pull dynamic is a psychological phenomenon that pushes someone away from one thing and pulls them closer to another. It initiates change in behaviour and is used in marketing to urge customers to adopt new solutions to their problems.**

When Tesla first floated the idea of an electric car sports car, they knew they would have to change people's minds. To move people away from the cars they were used to, Tesla would need to persuade customers that electric cars could be attractive, practical and perform well. Tesla's first test for their Roadster model in 2003 was a pretotype using the overlay method, where they modified a Lotus Elise. They asked interested customers to put down a $5,000 deposit and got several hundred deposits, which confirmed they had a desired product in the market.

Alan Clement, the founder of Revealed, a market research firm that works with Google, HubSpot and Netgear, says businesses must be aware of push and pull interdependencies when it comes to marketing and selling solutions. In his blog, "The Forces of Progress", he says that Tesla uses these interdependencies to attract customers. Tesla created pull by designing attractive cars to change people's minds and established its perception as a high-end car manufacturer. After 12 years of operations, in 2015, Tesla announced its first low-end electric car, the Model 3, and because they already had a pull dynamic in the industry, they got 325,000 pre-orders within the first week for a car that customers had neither seen nor driven yet.

The push-pull dynamic establishes the psychological reasoning behind your customer choosing your solution over your competitors.

- Push factors are things that make a customer unhappy about their current solution and consider an alternative solution — ineffectiveness, higher price and time-consuming. Think of the pain points from your customer's journey map. These are the push factors wanting them to consider other options.

- Pull factors are those that will pull the customer towards your product or solution. Think of the 'Desire — I wish statements' from the customer journey map. If you solve for these, they will become pull factors for your solution and make your customer choose you over the other.

Don't forget to also consider these interdependencies the other way around.

- Push factors for your products could be the credibility of your business because it's new.

- Pull factors that the customer has for their current solution could be the comfort of a known provider and the habit of using that product or service.

Once you've understood the push-pull dynamic from both sides, you can use it to craft the right marketing and positioning messages to attract your customer to your pretotype. More about that in the next few sections of this chapter.

EXERCISE 30: LIST PUSH-PULL FACTORS

List the push-pull dynamic with two to three competitors you have in the market today. Start by using your customer's current alternative from your customer journey map. I've used the toy library as an example below.

	What pushes your customer away from...	**What pulls your customer towards...**
Toy library (**your solution**)	• fear of unknown • trust	• ease of use & access • free delivery • low monthly fee • less hassles due to personalisation • streamlined process
Facebook groups (**current solution**)	• time-consuming • hand-overs with strangers • no guarantees • no way of knowing if toys are available or sold	• friends & peers • known platform • big company • used toys for less $

(Contd.)

Toy store (current solution)	• time-consuming • can't access after hours • higher prices • buy unnecessary toys	• can touch & feel quality • good variety • someone to ask & help • reputed • takes returns

As you can see, some of the pull factors for your competitors may not even be about the product itself. It is more about psychological safety — like a known platform, many people using it, reputation, etc. Craft your messages in a way that creates the perception of the push-pull dynamic in your favour.

Copy and creatives

'The pen is mightier than the sword,' as the old saying goes. Being able to craft messages that resonate with your audience will make a huge difference in the number of people that move through the AIDA funnel from the awareness stage into the other stages.

Effective messaging plays a big role in how your customers respond to you. There are two key things when it comes to creating marketing messages — copy and creatives.

- Copy is the words you write for your posts, ads or flyers.
- Creatives are the visual content like images and videos.

Copy and creatives are the medium by which you will communicate your message to your audience. They are your customer's first glimpse of your solution. You don't want to get this wrong.

You could use one or both in your marketing messages. Visual content is very attractive when done well. Words, on the other hand, can inspire action. So, build your copy and creatives keeping in mind all that you know about your customer. At this stage, four to five different types of copy and creatives are enough. You can mix and match to use across various platforms.

You can use copy and creatives in many ways, so don't limit your thinking to social media platforms. You can use them in flyers, posters, emails, text messages, landing pages and many more. You must also reuse them where possible and not recreate them every time — otherwise it's just time-consuming. Remember to always be succinct and clear in your messages.

Tips for good copy

- Good copy has three key things, all of which you have already gathered in the last few chapters:
  o the problem statement and pain points from the customer's lens
  o the value proposition that your solution delivers to them
  o the call to action that compels them to visit your landing page or video.
- Keep your copy as conversational as possible. Customers can sense when you are being robotic and transactional versus authentic and warm.
- Use storytelling where possible and keep it punchy.
- Create a sense of curiosity and make them want to know more.

William Siebler, the Managing Director of Cash Copy, shares great advice from his 30 years of experience as a persuasive copywriting expert and marketing guru in Australia. He says, "The best copy is written to just one person. So, when you sit down to write, have someone in mind and write to them. Write as you would talk to them and your copy will be far more natural and believable. Make sure you have one specific action in mind you want them to take and remember to ask them to do that. For bonus points, read your copy aloud to find bits that don't flow and then rewrite those bits."

Tips for effective creatives

- Your audience must be able to resonate with your creatives, so make sure the images and the video snippets you use are reflective of your target audience. Consider things like age, gender and culture when depicting them.

- Keep any text to a minimum on your images and videos as you will use copy and creatives together in most places. Make sure it sparks an emotion.

While you are at it, don't forget to create a company name and a logo to look professional.

EXERCISE 31: DESIGN COPY AND CREATIVES

1. Write your copy

Write 4–5 copy options of 100–150 words each. I recommend writing your own copy first. Even if you decide to engage a copywriter at some point, writing your own copy at this stage will help you learn what kind of messaging works and what doesn't. No one understands your customer like you do. After all the work you have done so far, you are best placed to articulate what your customer wants. A copywriter will need direction from you to help them write the most effective copy. So first give it a go and then you can hire someone to polish it up.

There are many copywriting tools available online to help you with this task. You could even ask someone in your network to help. We will look at crafting irresistible offers in the next chapter, which will be further refinement of your copy from here.

2. Make your creatives

Make 4–5 creative options that can go with your copy. You may have made some for your landing page already, which you can reuse. If you haven't made any yet, a good place to start is canva.com. You can pick a template and modify it to suit your solution. Canva also gives you options to create videos with existing templates. You could use those or go back to some of the suggestions from the video explainer method in the previous chapter.

Organic and inorganic marketing

There are two ways to market your solution. First is the organic way, which is a slow but sure pathway to create awareness. Examples of organic marketing are word of mouth and regular social media posts. Then there's the inorganic way, where you spend money to reach your target audience faster. This is also called paid marketing and includes paid social media ads, banners and billboards.

The choice of your pathway will depend on two things:

- how fast you want to create awareness in the market and drive people to your landing page or videos (this is called driving traffic)
- how deep your pockets are (in other words, how much money you are willing to spend).

To be visible to hundreds and thousands of people, you must use a higher proportion of inorganic marketing. While this pathway is more expensive than organic marketing, it is the quickest way to know if your idea has value in the market.

Both organic and inorganic marketing have their advantages and disadvantages as outlined on the next page.

	Organic marketing	**Inorganic marketing**
Advantages	• authentic • builds followership • creates organic authority • good for building reputation and loyalty • low on cost	• targeted towards ideal customers • can drive large amount of traffic • builds rapid awareness • low effort compared to organic • capability to retarget your customers so they see your ads over and over • analytics capability
Disadvantages	• slow • low return on investment at first • broad in reach and not targeted • high effort	• more expensive • sometimes makes people sceptical about a product or service being pushed on them

At this stage, a mix of organic and inorganic marketing is the best approach. You must build some credibility with your customers through consistent organic posts. This gives you a long-term benefit. For the short term, inorganic ads will give you a great return on investment. With as little as $50 to $100, you can reach thousands of people who are in your target market.

EXERCISE 32: POSITION YOUR EXPERIMENTS IN THE MARKET

To put your marketing in action, choose the copy and creatives that you will use for your different marketing pathways.

For organic marketing:

1. Reach out via email to your 25 interviewees from Chapter Five.

2. Create some social media posts on a regular basis to reach your own networks.

3. Tell people you meet about what you do.

4. Ask friends and family to spread the word for you.

5. If you know anyone in your extended networks who may be your ideal customer, call them and let them know as well.

For inorganic marketing, use the platforms your ideal customers use and explore how you can create paid ads. Most social media platforms allow paid ads, and the process is simple with step-by-step instructions available on their websites.

At Jumpstart Studio, we help clients with the end-to-end of positioning and marketing their early-stage ideas and experiments. However, going deeper into the art of creating marketing ads is beyond the purview of this book.

IN SUMMARY . . .

- In this chapter, you've learned how, when and where to position yourself and your solution so that you have the maximum chance of success. Now it's time to stop working behind the scenes and start putting your solution out in the market.

- The concepts on positioning you have learned in this chapter show you the easiest path to marketing your solution. Now get out there and start being the entrepreneur you were born to be.

- In the next chapter, you will learn how to get your first paying customers — the biggest moment in your business journey that you will never forget.

RESOURCES

You can download the Customer Journey Mapping template from this chapter on my website www.jumpstartstudio.com.au

Chapter Nine

Get Paying Customers

Paying customers are the ultimate validation that your business idea is worth pursuing. It is the culmination of all the hard work you have done in the last few chapters. It is that exciting moment in your business journey that you will remember for a long time to come. It is a green light that your idea has value in the market and there are people willing to pay for it.

This chapter is about the first paying customer paradigm. Understanding what makes your first paying customer valuable and what inherent risks they carry will help you keep your eye on the final goal: your profitable customers. In a Forbes article, "The First Customers are the Hardest: Top Founders Discuss the Challenges of Getting Initial Traction", John Rampton, the founder of online payments company, Due, and productivity company, Calendar, says that your first five to ten paying customers are invaluable. You can't put a price tag on them as they mean so much more than the revenue that they provide. From your first few customers, you will learn what it takes to get them to buy, how much they are willing to pay and why they're interested in your service. In addition, these first customers show that your product is valuable, which demonstrates to your potential investor that your idea has some validity.

In this chapter, you will build further from the positioning work you did in the last chapter to give your solution the best chances of success and to get your first paying customers. You will learn:

- the key aspects of pricing your solution and presenting it to your customer with an irresistible offer
- how to deliver your solution to your customers
- the value of iterative testing
- how to recognise and extract value from all kinds of first paying customers, even if they are not your ideal customers.

Pricing

One of the biggest dilemmas founders have is how to price their solution. What is the right price to charge your customers? How do you make money from your idea? I see founders spend hours on this topic. Abdo Riani, the CEO of a startup development company called VisionX Partners, sums it up in his Forbes article, "How to Price Your Early Stage Startup". He says, "For many entrepreneurs, pricing is as complicated as advanced calculus. But unlike math, there is not only one correct answer to the pricing problem." He explains that underpricing, overpricing or not charging when customers are willing to pay is a huge disservice to your business and to the customer. It can have many repercussions like lower revenue, lost customers, or even startup failure.

> **Having an effective pricing strategy drives your startup profits, but it also generates higher customer retention and satisfaction.**

Price is one of the most important considerations customers make when paying for a product or service. But many entrepreneurs struggle to price their products well. At this early stage when you haven't yet built your product, it can be hard to estimate how you should price your solution. Lucky for you, I have a rule of thumb for first-time founders. And it works. Every. Single. Time.

At this stage, your aim is not to make a profit. You will learn more about how to make a profit in the next chapter. So, make it as easy as possible for your ideal customer to choose your product or service. No, this doesn't mean you offer it for free. But you must lower the price barrier enough so that people want to pay. And keep it high enough so that it doesn't look like a scam.

There are many different pricing strategies in the market, but at this stage, two are relevant for you.

1. **Market pricing or competition pricing** – In this strategy, you consider pricing close to where your current competitors are priced.

Think of what your customer pays today to solve the problem. Look at a few different competitors. Price your solution in the same range, a bit lower if you can.

2. **Value-based pricing** – This type of pricing is good if you have a value proposition that far exceeds your competitors. This type of pricing reflects what your customers perceive about your solution. This type of pricing develops over time when you are able to gather customer feedback on your experiments.

EXERCISE 33: PRICE YOUR SOLUTION

In this exercise, we will look at how you can apply the market pricing strategy. To do this, you must first identify what your customers pay for the solution they use today. Consider pricing from direct competitors — similar products or services. And indirect competitors — alternative solutions that people use today.

Let's look at this using our toy library example:

- Direct competitors are other toy libraries which charge a monthly subscription fee of, let's say, $60.

- From our hypothetical interviews, we know that Sara spends about $50 a month on average on toys from Facebook — our indirect competitor.

- This gives an indication that if the price point is between $40 and $60 a month, it would be on par with the market rates.

- This would be good enough to get Sara to consider the solution as a new alternative to what she does today.

Now it's your turn.

1. Research your competition

Take some time to investigate your competition, both direct and indirect.

2. Review customer interviews

Review data from your customer interviews to gauge what price they would be willing to pay for your solution.

3. Decide your price

Based on this information, decide the best price point for your product or service.

Crafting irresistible offers

In Australia, 26th December, Boxing Day, is one of the most awaited days of the year (after Christmas day, of course). The Boxing Day Test Match is a tradition for Australian cricket fans, which is played between Australia and another national team on this day. It is one of the most anticipated sporting events of the year. Another big tradition is the Boxing Day sales. Businesses, big and small, vie for the left-over Christmas dollars from customers by offering huge discounts and offers on products. They open earlier than usual to allow for longer shopping times. Some large department stores like Myer have customers lining up at the door from as early as 4am to be the first to get in. People perceive that they are going to snag some great value for their money at the Boxing Day sales. On the other hand, businesses ensure that they deliver irresistible offers to their customers to make it worthwhile.

"An irresistible offer is simply a strategic structuring of your products and/or services, where the value-to-cost ratio is value-heavy. Meaning, that the value of your offer far exceeds the cost to access the value," says Michael R Hunter, the founder of PersonalBrand.com. Hunter is the branding expert for some of this decade's biggest influencers, including author Brendon Burchard, business expert Mel Abraham, and memory expert Jim Kwik. In his view, when a customer comes across your offer, it must trigger the response, "Wow, this is an absolute no-brainer. I must buy this right now." It must be so good that they can't say no. They can't resist it.

Offers are the way to convert medium-value data from customers into high-value data — money. In Chapter Seven, you established the data you want to collect from your customers through your experiments.

- If you've gone straight for the high-value data — collecting a monetary deposit or the full price for your product or service upfront — that's great. You will still need an offer on your landing page or one that you can communicate to your customer.

- If you are collecting medium-value data in your experiments, like an email address or contact information, then there is an additional step in converting that medium-value data into money. In this case, you will send your offer to the customer via emails. It might take a few emails to convert your customer into a paying customer.

In both cases, you will need to understand how to craft your offer for your customers. An offer is the final step before a customer becomes a paying customer. Just presenting a price to your customer, like businesses did in the past, is not good enough to convert people into paying customers. You must tell your customers why they must consider buying your solution. Help them make the decision to buy.

Without an irresistible offer, you leave a lot of the sales process to luck. Building your solution on luck and chance is the worst thing you can do for your business. It means you have no method to replicate your success. So, take some time to craft your irresistible offer. As with everything in business, creating offers is also a test and learn process. You will get the hang of what works and what doesn't as you keep creating the offers and keep testing with your target market.

EXERCISE 34: CRAFT YOUR IRRESISTIBLE OFFER

I have an eight-step irresistible offer framework that works well for most businesses.

Your offer must clearly explain or include the following:

1. Clarity – in the value you provide to your customer and how you are addressing their needs.

2. Advantage – why your customer must switch over to you from their current solution.

3. Price – the dollar value of the offer compared to the dollar value of the product or service at regular times (if they are different).

4. Scarcity – limited availability of the product or service at this price.

5. Urgency – time limit until when the offer is available, to prompt immediate action.

6. Guarantee – a money-back guarantee over a few days or weeks provides assurance.

7. A call to action – such as a 'buy now' button. Make sure the button leads the customer to a payment page to input their credit card details. You can use a payment provider like PayPal or Stripe to accept payments. You can learn more about how to do this on their websites at paypal.com and stripe.com. If you choose to set up a bank transfer method instead, make sure you check with your bank on the best way to set this up and integrate it with the buy now button on your email.

8. Testimonials – testimonials from existing customers are a great way to showcase some validation and build credibility with your customers. At this early stage of the business, you may not have any testimonials to show your customers, but as you start getting customers, don't forget to collect testimonials that you can showcase with your offer.

Let's use the toy library example to see how it works:

1. Clarity – one-stop access to used toys, low monthly subscription, free delivery and pickup of toys.

2. Advantage – option to buy toys at half price after trying them, free access to three-hour playgroups every weekend, weekly customised toy offers direct to email.

3. Price – pre-launch price of $10 for the first month, standard price of $40 per month.

4. Scarcity – pre-launch price only available to first ten customers.

5. Urgency – offer expires in three days.

6. Guarantee – no lock-in contract, 30-day money-back guarantee if you don't like the service.

7. A call to action – 'buy now' button on landing page with a prompt that says, 'Click here to make the first $10 payment and we will send you an information email with next steps'.

8. Testimonials – testimonials from existing customers.

Delivery

When we ran the first experiment for Foodtropia, although we hadn't built anything yet, we had a rough idea of how we would deliver the service — what resources we would need, how much it would cost us, what activities we needed to conduct. In most cases, you will know how to deliver the MVP of your solution within a few weeks of your experimentation. However, in some cases, like when you are building a technology solution or a new car like Tesla, you may need a longer time to deliver. For such cases, collect an initial deposit from your customers instead of the full payment upfront. Make sure you set clear expectations on the delivery timelines. Collect their email address and keep your customers updated on the progress. This creates credibility for your brand in the market and can also increase the perceived value of your product or service.

For any reason, if you do not intend to provide the solution after your experiment, do not collect money from your customers. You can still conduct your experiments as if you are going to collect high-value data from your customers. You can do this by using a dummy 'buy now' button that leads your customers to a customised 'thank you' page rather than a payment page. On the page, inform them that this was a test and request them to leave their email address so that you can contact them in the future when you have moved your solution to the next stage of development. It's always nice to give them something in return for their time if you can.

Whether the customer pays or takes the action to pay, either way, they have validated your idea for you. Money in your pocket is always better, but it is also important to be transparent about your own limitations when it comes to delivering the solution. Winning trust from your customers is an important part in making sure you and your business succeed. False claims can damage your personal and business reputation. Research shows that bad experiences and memories stick in our brains for longer. You don't want your brand and your name to conjure up bad memories for people. Many of your first customers will come from your own personal networks, which can have a longer-term impact.

EXERCISE 35: PLAN THE DELIVERY OF YOUR SOLUTION

The main purpose of your experiments is to collect data to see if customers are willing to buy your solution. If you aren't quite ready with your solution, identify and plan for how and when you will be ready. Create a delivery timeline and make it clear to your customers in the irresistible offer. For example, in the toy library scenario, we may not have purchased all the toys yet. In this case, estimate when you can have the toys ready and available, and feature that date in the irresistible offer.

Also remember, at this stage you only need to deliver an MVP. For the toy library example, if we are not able to offer home delivery to all locations at first, make this clear in your irresistible offer as well. Outline the areas where you will operate for now with a plan for the rest of the areas.

If you don't know how you are going to deliver at all, go back to your business model in Chapter Three. Look at the feasibility and viability sections.

- Has something changed given all the work you have done since then?

- What are some of the resources you have listed there? Are they available to you today?
- What partnerships do you need to deliver your product or services?
- Does your offer align with your business model?

Iterate

Entrepreneurship is all about understanding and applying the process of iteration and continuous improvement.

> **Failures and successes are not the destination; they are a part of the journey. Don't let them limit your business dreams.**

With Foodtropia, our first experiment was a success. We hosted a Spanish dinner party with strangers. We had five customers that night. They loved the whole experience we curated for them. They gave us valuable feedback and glowing reviews. We were chuffed. Our second experiment was a three-course Indian dinner and paired wine for $100 per person. We increased the price from our previous dinner, which was $50 per person, based on the feedback from customers. We sold out. We had six customers this time. Again, we got excellent reviews and feedback. We thought we had found a market and a business model that works. Our business was a huge success story.

But with the third, fourth and fifth dinners, we sold nothing. We replicated the process from our first and second dinners, yet we sold nothing. We were stumped. It had worked before, so why wasn't it working now? For dinner six, we again sold four tickets, and dinner seven we sold five tickets. We delivered those two dinners and got great reviews and feedback. But for dinner eight, we just sold two tickets and didn't reach our threshold. We returned the money to the customers and cancelled the dinner. They wouldn't have had the experience they paid for, and it wasn't viable for us to host the dinner.

What this told us is that we were onto something, but we still had some work to do. This is where iteration and continuous improvement comes in. It lets you see the gaps in what you're doing and not just rely on the first paying customers as the best validation of your idea. Our mistake with Foodtropia was that we didn't improve or change things on the iterations we did. We tried to replicate our initial success, which meant we were relying more on chance than on a proper strategy.

The lesson there is that even if you have initial success with your experiments, don't stop there. Keep iterating and testing out different combinations of things. A winning formula is a sum of its different parts. To identify the parts, run multiple experiments. Position them in multiple ways. Keep testing the different assumptions you have made. But do it one assumption at a time so you know what works and what doesn't.

Depending on how well you have conducted your business-building steps so far, you may get your first paying customer with your first experiment. If you do, well done. But the buck doesn't stop there. You need more than one paying customer to succeed. This concept is called 'traction' in startup language.

Continuous improvement is the fundamental principle of iteration. If it takes a few tries to get your first paying customer, don't be disheartened. You're building a business for the long run — and that is not an easy job. The key to success is to keep iterating and testing the market with different experiments, positioning strategies and offers.

> **Learning from what doesn't work is just as important as building on what does.**

EXERCISE 36: ITERATE AND REFINE YOUR SOLUTION

1. Track progress

Once you've created your first experiment and positioned it in the market, track its progress for a few days. Your first customers are most likely to come from your existing network of people who know and trust you — friends, family, and the first 25 people you spent time interviewing in Chapter Five.

2. Create your experiment list

Create a list of all the different experiments you can create for your solution and the corresponding list of where you can position it to reach your customers.

3. Schedule your experiments

Create a timeline with dates for when you will run these experiments — how many days, what data will you collect and the thresholds to measure success.

Remember, your aim in this process is to collect high-value data in different ways — actual money or a deposit from your customers — and to learn what works well and what doesn't so you can keep tweaking your solution.

False positives

A false-positive means a paying customer who doesn't have the problem you're trying to solve but still buys from you. Sometimes false positives come in the form of well-meaning friends and family. Other times, it may be people who want to try out your solution once, but never come back as repeat customers.

Awareness of the types of paying customers your business attracts is a huge game-changer. Think of the times that you have been a false-positive customer for other businesses. How many times have you signed up for a service and cancelled after the trial period or after the first few months? Why did you not continue with the service? On the other hand, how many other services do you continue to use and pay for? Think about everyday services, on-demand TV subscriptions, grocery delivery services and music streaming services. You pay because they solve something for you.

When we started hosting dinners for Foodtropia, people in our network were very excited to try our service. It's not uncommon that your friends and family will want to support you. Our target market was people who are curious about other cultures and want to meet other like-minded strangers. But since some of our friends were happy to pay for the dinners, we welcomed them. They were people who loved us but didn't fall into our ideal customer bucket. Or so we thought. The advantage for us though was that they could help us reach more people through word of mouth after experiencing our dinners. We deemed them as our false positives. We had about one or two false positives at most dinners.

However, as we started having deeper conversations with everyone at the dinner parties, we learned why people were paying to come to these dinners. We learned that the problem we were solving for our customers was far more personal than cultural curiosity. It was loneliness. We discovered that many of our friends, who we deemed as false positives, had the same problem as our ideal customers. Their reason to be at those dinners was the same as those of the strangers. They were lonely too and that's why they came to our dinners, not just to support us.

We found that our dinners attracted two distinct personas. People in their 30s who were single or didn't have kids like their other friends, and didn't know where to find new like-minded friends. And people in their 60s whose kids had grown up and left home. They now had more time on their hands and were looking for new experiences.

Our false positives were also our ideal customers, we just didn't know at the time. So having false positives is not a bad thing. You might uncover an opportunity that you didn't know exists. It will allow you to tweak your solution to better suit this new customer segment you have uncovered. This tweaking is called 'pivoting' in startup jargon.

EXERCISE 37: IDENTIFY YOUR FALSE POSITIVES

You will come across false-positive customers as you test and iterate. These are paying customers that are not from your target market, but you see them wanting your solution and buying from you often. If you find that you get a large proportion of false positives in every iteration as compared to your expected target market, then there are two things you must do.

1. Find out what is attracting these false-positive customers

- Talk to them and conduct a customer discovery process.
- Use the empathy map from Chapter Six to chart their responses.
- Find out if there's a common reason by identifying patterns.
- Make a pivot. Go back to your Business Model from Chapter Three and see how you can connect the dots and tweak your solution to serve this segment.

2. Identify why you are not attracting your target market

Understanding why your expected ideal customers are not attracted to your solution will help you decide if you should make a pivot. Go back to your 25 interviewees from Chapter Five. Talk to them and find out what is stopping them from adopting your solution.

IN SUMMARY . . .

- In this chapter, you have learned how to price your solution, create irresistible offers, and iterate on your experiments to attract paying customers.

- Paying customers are invaluable to your business. While they may not pay you much now, just the fact that they are willing to pay something for your ideas and a very first experimental version of your solution, is massive validation that you must keep pursuing your idea.

- You will always remember your first paying customer. It's like when you got paid your first salary. It may not have been much, but you still remember who you worked for and how you felt when that money hit your bank account or your hand.

- The goal for any business is to make a profit. Having paying customers is the first step in making your business profitable. In the next chapter, I will show you how to go from paying customers to making a profit. The point in time where you become a true entrepreneur.

Chapter Ten

Make a Profit

First, I want to congratulate you. I speak to many aspiring founders every week, but very few have the courage to make their dreams come true.

> **If you have taken the steps outlined in this book so far, you are in the top 5% of people who are chasing their business dreams. Kudos.**

Building a business is not easy, but it is fun and very fulfilling. If you embody the entrepreneurial spirit and use some strategic moves I've shown you in this book, you will enjoy the journey.

The last nine chapters focus on the two most important things your business needs to succeed: you and your customer. You have figured out your sweet spot, put some safety nets in place, understood your customer's needs, challenges and desires. You have designed your solution for them and learned to experiment and test your solutions in the market. You have worked out the quickest way to start generating revenue and delivering your solution. Now it's time to see how you can make your paying customers profitable ones.

Most people fear the accounting and financial side of the business. I have a master's degree in accounting, and I can vouch that business accounting can become complex. There are many books and professionals out there who will be able to help you. I recommend you engage professional help early in your journey to support you with your business finances. However, to have meaningful conversations with your accountant you must know the basics. Founders who learn, embrace and own their numbers have a higher chance of success. There is also a lot of jargon in accounting, but once you understand the basics, as I will show you in this chapter, you will be set to make the right financial decisions.

This chapter is the most complex chapter in this book. It is also one of the most important chapters when it comes to preventing your failure early in the business-building process. As you saw in Chapter One and Chapter Two, the second highest reason businesses fail is due to financial mismanagement. Profit takes patience, persistence and a plan. Be patient and continue to persist with your business activities. But how long before you make a profit? To answer that question, you must have a plan — a plan to work out how and when paying customers can start becoming profitable.

Planning for profit is one of the most valuable things you can do to ensure you don't become a part of the failure statistics. Most businesses take time to become profitable, yet most first-time founders fall into the chasm of financial mismanagement because they expect profits too soon and don't know how to plan for the profits. Profit isn't as simple as it seems, but this chapter will give you sufficient information to start having the right conversations with your accountant, bookkeepers, bankers and investors. Understanding and applying the concepts in this chapter is the difference between your business flying or failing.

Tony Robbins, the famous motivational speaker and author, says "You wouldn't fly a plane without knowing how to read the gauges – and the same applies to business". On his blog, "How to Make a Profit: 11 Expert Strategies for Building a Profitable Business", he says, "You can't tell if you are winning or losing if you don't understand the controls. Being able to read a balance sheet, income statement and cash flow statement, means you'll be able to participate fully in conversations about how to make a profit." He also says that while you may hear of success stories about new businesses making heaps of money overnight, the reality is often very different. For new companies, the first challenge is to figure out if they can even stay open. Then they need to understand what it takes to make a profit. And then it takes them years to learn how to make profits. Uber is a classic example. It started over a decade ago and has never reported a profit. They have made a net loss of over US $22 billion so far according to a *Financial Times* report from June 2021.

In this chapter, you will build on the work you've done in the last nine chapters by looking further into the problem-solution fit and the product-market fit. Then you will learn to create an indicative profit and loss (P&L) projection, which is your plan to profitability. You will also understand some success metrics and metrics that investors look for — like break-even point, retention rate and churn rate. And you will learn about the concept of ramen profitability, which is one of the fastest ways for startups to become profitable.

Find the right fit

Creating a profit in business is like solving a puzzle. It's about finding the right pieces that fit together and having fun along the way. Fit is the magic word when it comes to creating sustainable businesses. There are two types of fit you must consider:

1. The problem-solution fit, where you have identified the right solution that fits the customer's needs.

2. The product-market fit, where you start seeing a steady flow of paying customers for your product or service.

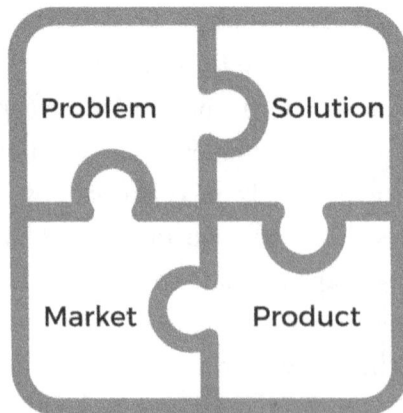

Think of it as the pieces of a puzzle. Not all pieces will fit together, but the right ones will. Achieving fit in business is much the same — the right solution will fit the problem and the right product or service will fit the market. Only then will your business make money. Without a market that wants and pays for your product on an ongoing basis, you can't generate a profit.

In the last nine chapters of this book, you have been solving for these two fits. You started with the problem-solution fit through your customer discovery and insights creation work, and moved into finding the product-market fit through your experiments and testing in the last few chapters.

Product-market fit can differ, depending on what type of product or service you are selling. You must measure product-market fit on two things:

- the flow of new customers
- the regularity of returning customers.

Let's look at how this differs from different types of products or services.

If you're developing a hardware product like headphones, you can't expect to have the same customer buying from you every month. Nobody needs new headphones every month. The regularity of returning customers may be once every year or once every two years. In that case, you must attract new customers all the time. You will know if you have a product-market fit when you see a steady flow of customers for a set period. For example, 50 new customers every month for the next three months shows product-market fit.

On the other hand, a service business like home delivery of groceries may need to consider steady flow of new paying customers and regularity of returning customers each month to evaluate their product-market fit. The interval could be shorter for some other businesses. As you can see from these examples, product-market fit is subject to the type of product or service and the type of market you serve.

Achieving product-market fit might take a while. So, before you start worrying about making a profit, allow yourself a few months to get on track for product-market fit. After all, if you don't have a market, you don't have a business. Set a measure of success like the number of returning customers and new customers every month. Once you achieve it, you are ready to start making and measuring profits. The rest of this chapter will show you how to do that.

Profit and loss projections

The financial health of your business is much like your personal health. For example, how do you know if your blood pressure is too high or too low, or if your cholesterol is within a healthy range, or if you're overweight? Your health is measured in numbers. To improve your health, you must know what your numbers are and what they mean against benchmarks. You must also identify the levers to pull, like changing your lifestyle or using medication. The same goes with your business. Knowing if your idea works for the market is half the battle in building a successful business. The other half is to make it profitable. To do this, you must know your numbers. You don't have to be an accountant, but you must understand the basic concepts of profit and loss, what underlying factors affect them and the levers that you can pull to make your business perform better.

The three key financial statements your business needs are:

- Profit & loss statement – also called an income statement, this outlines the income and expenses of your business to determine how much profit or loss your business is making.

- Balance sheet – this document shows all that the business owns (assets), owes (liabilities) and has received as investments (equity). It shows the financial status of a business at a point in time.

- Cash flow statement – this is used to track and manage all the cash inflows and outflows in the business related to its operations and investments. It differs from the profit and loss statement as it tracks all the financial activity in a business, not only the income and expenses.

Most businesses get these financial statements in place within a year or so of operations. Prasoon Veerath, a Chartered Accountant and Group Director at

Carisma Solutions, says that in addition to these three financial statements, you will need to consider creating a budget (also called a spending plan) for your business to operate once you know the kind of cash inflows and outflows your business can generate. In his 14 years of experience working with businesses, Veerath has seen that founders who focus on the financial targets as key performance indicators for their business and track them regularly perform better and stay in business longer than others. So get professional help to put these statements in place.

At this early stage in your business, focus on setting a benchmark for your financial performance first. To do this, use a method called projections. A projection helps you forecast what your financial performance could look like in the future. Then, as your business delivers the solution in the market, you can track your performance against the projection on a regular basis and identify where improvements are required.

If you don't have a projection in place, you have nothing to track against or even know if your business is making a profit.

While there are a few different types of projections a business needs such as a sales forecast and payroll forecast, first start with a simple profit and loss (P&L) projection.

A P&L projection forecasts two main things:

- the revenue you generate by selling your solution (income)
- the costs you incur in operating the business (expenses), measured at regular intervals (e.g., monthly or quarterly).

A short-term P&L projection is between one and three years, while a long-term P&L projection is between three and five years. For now, a short-term projection will suffice; once you are able to meet your short-term projection numbers, you can then start planning for the long term. Since most early-stage businesses start making a profit after 18 to 24 months of operations, it is best to do a two-year (24-month) projection to start. It lets you understand when and how your business will make a profit. It also allows you to plan for things like seasonality and financial year ends.

To build a meaningful projection, you must base it on realistic numbers. So, once you start selling your solution and seeing some early traction, you can start building your projection. You may still have to make many assumptions and guess the numbers at this stage, but that is okay. You will revisit your projection every month to update it with the actual — the real revenue and costs that you incur each month. You will find differences between the actuals and the forecast numbers. This is called a variance. If your actuals are better than your forecast — higher revenue and lower costs — you have a positive variance. The inverse is a negative variance. If your variance in any given month is more than 10% or you see a variance continue over two consecutive months, analyse it. If it was due to a one-off event, make a note. But if you expect it to be an ongoing variance due to a hike in supply prices or change in your sales price, you must adjust the rest of your projection to reflect this.

EXERCISE 38: BUILD A P&L PROJECTION

You will need a spreadsheet to build your P&L projection. There's a template available on the Jumpstart Studio website that you can download and use.

Before you build a P&L projection, you must understand a few key numbers first. Take the toy library, for example.

1. **Revenue (also called income)** – is the money you make by selling a product or service. Revenue is the number of units you expect to sell each month multiplied by the price per unit.

   Let's say the monthly subscription fee is $40 for your toy library. You enrol at least 20 customers like Sara in the first month. Your revenue for the month is 20 times $40, which is $800.

2. **Costs (also called expenses)** – all the costs that you incur in running your business. There are three types to consider here.

   i.   **Variable costs** – those that change with every unit you produce. For example, raw materials, hourly wages and commissions. For the toy library, this could be the credit card fees to bank or payment platforms like PayPal, and packaging and delivery costs.

  ii.   **Fixed costs** – those that remain fixed every month, irrespective of the number of units you produce. They may change over time but they do not vary monthly. Common examples of this are rent, insurance and staff salaries. For the toy library which you intend to operate from home to start with, some of these are landing page costs, marketing and advertising costs, phone, electricity and insurance.

 iii.   **Depreciation & amortisation costs (if any)** – these relate to costs of your tangible, depreciable assets like machinery, land, inventory and vehicle, and intangible amortisable assets such as patents, trademarks and software. These are costs that can be spread over the lifetime of the asset. Unlike the Variable and Fixed costs, the company doesn't suffer any cash reduction due to these costs. These are used for accounting purposes.

3. **Earnings before interest and tax (EBIT)** – also known as operating profit, EBIT is your revenue minus your costs.

4. **Tax and interest expense** – the tax your business pays and the interest you pay on any loans in the business.

5. **Net profit (or loss)** – your operating profit minus your interest and tax.

It is common for businesses to forecast a net loss for the first 12 to 18 months of operations. Make sure you know how you can keep funding the business during this period without going into a massive personal debt. Focus more on the levers that affect your profit and loss at this stage to make sure that you've taken all the pieces into consideration when calculating your revenues and costs.

A P&L projection is not a set-and-forget activity. You must update your projection often to reflect your business' reality. The best practice is to do it every month.

Projections are also tied into all the work you have done in this book so far. Remember the financial runway exercise from Chapter Two (Exercise 10) where you identified how long you can make your money last in business? Use that as a yardstick to build your projections. Your projections should also reflect your business model from Chapter Three. So, make sure you don't do this activity in isolation.

Success metrics

Every business must track a few key metrics to determine if they are successful in the market or not. As an entrepreneur, you must know these metrics because they help you:

- make financially viable decisions from the start
- set benchmarks and targets to achieve in your business to make it profitable
- have meaningful conversations with investors and other business partners in the future.

Here are three metrics that will start you off on the right foot.

1. **Break-even point (BEP)** – to be profitable, every business must sell a minimum number of units of their products or services. This is called BEP. Knowing this number helps you set the right sales and revenue targets for your business.

2. **Retention rate** – this is the percentage of customers who continue to stay with your business from one period to another. A high retention rate means your product or service has a high value in the market and your customers love your business. Investors favour businesses with high retention rates.

3. **Churn rate** – the opposite of retention rate, churn rate is the percentage of customers who leave your business from one period to another. A high churn rate indicates that your business idea is not hitting the mark and you have more work to do when it comes to customer discovery and designing your solution.

I will show you how to calculate these for your business in the exercise below. These calculations are also built into the downloadable P&L projection template on the Jumpstart Studio website.

EXERCISE 39: CALCULATE YOUR SUCCESS METRICS

1. Calculate BEP

$$BEP = \frac{Fixed\ costs}{Contribution\ margin}$$

where, contribution margin is price per unit - variable cost per unit

From the P&L projection for the toy library example, let's say:

- Fixed cost is $1,000 a month
- Price per unit (subscription fee) is $40 per month
- Variable cost per subscription is $21

Contribution margin = $40 - $21 =$19

BEP = $1,000/$19 = 53

This indicates that the toy library will need to have 53 paying subscribers per month to break even. It will start making a profit from the 54th customer onwards.

If you vary any of the levers such as price per unit, fixed costs or variable costs, the BEP will change. For example if you increase price per unit or reduce fixed costs and variable costs, the BEP will be lower.

2. Calculate retention rate

Retention = Customers at end - New customers gained
(in a given period)

$$Retention\ rate = \frac{Retention}{Customers\ at\ start\ of\ period} \times 100\%$$

For the toy library example, let's say for one month:

- *Customers at the start of the month = 20*
- *New customers gained in the month = 5*
- *Customers lost in the month = 3*
- *Customers at the end of the month = 22*

Retention = (22-5) = 17

Retention rate = 17/20 = 0.85 $\times$ 100% = 85%

Retention rates can be tracked weekly, monthly, quarterly or annually, depending on the type of business you operate and the regularity of customers you expect. In this example, there is an 85% retention rate, which means 85% of existing customers continue to stay with the business from one month to another. While a high retention rate is good, it is always best to benchmark against industry standards. Most industries have retention rates between 60-90%.

3. Calculate churn rate

$$Churn\ rate = 1 - Retention\ rate$$

Using the same example from above,

Churn rate = 1 - 85% = 15%

In this example, the churn rate indicates that the business has lost 15% of its customers in this month. As your retention rate drops, your churn rates will keep increasing, however if your churn rates surpass your retention rates, it is a sign that you need to tweak something in your business. As outlined in the above example, the best thing to do is to conduct customer discovery and learn why your customers are choosing to leave your business.

Ramen profitability

The most common question first-time founders ask me is, "When can I pay myself a salary?"

In January 2009, Brian Chesky, the co-founder of Airbnb, sent an email to Paul Graham, an entrepreneur and venture capitalist who co-founded Y-combinator, the influential startup accelerator and early-stage seed capital firm. As one of the participants at Y-combinator, Chesky was reporting to Graham with their earnings that week. Graham shared this email in 2020 on Twitter. They had made $734 that week but had worked out that they needed to be making $1,000 per week to be 'ramen profitable'.

Ramen profitability is a concept popularised by Paul Graham in the late 2000s. It means making a startup profitable while its founders live on a ramen budget. Here, ramen refers to the inexpensive instant noodles from Japan. The biggest advantage to ramen profitability is that you are no longer at the mercy of investors. You use the money generated by the business to run the business. If you choose to raise investment from external investors, you will get better terms because you are not dependent on them. There have been many cases where startups have been in desperate need of money and have been taken advantage of by investors. Think of the popular TV show "Shark Tank" where prominent business investors try to negotiate terms with startup founders who need funding. The more in need of money you are, the more pliable you become.

On the other hand, being profitable makes you attractive to investors. It shows them that you can manage their two biggest worries — growing your customers and handling your finances. Investors fund smart founders operating scalable businesses in big markets. Yet many fail. The two biggest mistakes they make, as you saw in Chapter One, are making things nobody needs and running out of money. Becoming ramen profitable proves that you are avoiding these mistakes.

EXERCISE 40: AIM FOR RAMEN PROFITABILITY

So, for a start, determine how much salary you need for the most basic living expenses. Add this in your profit and loss projection as a salary. It is not unusual for founders to sustain themselves on their savings for the first year of the business until they have some regular cash flow. If you take a basic salary from the second year onwards, would you remain profitable? If not, what levers can you use to become ramen profitable? Adjust your profit and loss projection to reflect that.

Remember, this is not going to be the salary you will take in the future, nor is it advisable to be on a ramen diet for years on end. I recommend you replace ramen with something healthier, even from the start. Soup, salads or simple home-cooked meals. As Graham says, "A startup's destination is to grow really big. Ramen profitability is a trick for not dying en route."

IN SUMMARY . . .

You are now on your way to making your business a profitable one. It takes some learning, planning and persistence. Numbers are not someone else's business; you must know your numbers to have the right conversations with the right people to create a successful business of your dreams.

RESOURCES

You can download the P&L projection template from this chapter on my website www.jumpstartstudio.com.au to build your indicative projections, calculate BEP and other success metrics. Always seek professional advice to ensure your projections and the calculations are right for your business. The information on the template is a starting point and indicative only.

Conclusion: Make it happen

The world needs more entrepreneurs — people who have the courage to step out of their comfort zone and embark on a journey of adventure and curiosity. People who have the burning desire to make their dreams a reality. People who want to help others and make this world a better place. People like you.

At the core of it all, entrepreneurs are creators with the power to change the world for the better. Like you, there are others out there embarking on this journey. In 2021, 'the great resignation' gripped most of the large economies of the world. The US Bureau of Labour Statistics reported four million Americans quit their job in July 2021 alone. On the other hand, 4.35 million new businesses opened in 2020, which was a 24% increase from the previous year according to the US Business Formation Statistics. In Australia, the number of small businesses in 2020–21 rose by almost 88,000 according to the Australian Bureau of Statistics.

If you've done all I've asked you to do in this book, you've come a long way from sitting at your desk and wondering how to start a business. You are now well on your way to becoming a successful entrepreneur with paying customers and a profitable business. For now, take a moment to stop, look back to where you were before you began this journey and think about how far you've come in just a few months. Reward yourself for staying the course and being committed to making your dreams a reality.

Like I said in Chapter One, ideas don't cost you a penny, but neither do they make you a dollar. With almost eight billion people in this world as of 2021, imagine how many brilliant business ideas are born every single day. Not all of them become brilliant businesses. Why? The difference is a six-letter word: action.

Action is the difference between ideas and reality. Action is the difference between thinking about climbing Mount Everest and standing at the peak. In this book, I've shown you the easiest way to take action to make your ideas a reality.

> **It's the small steps you take today that will amount to the big leap you've been afraid of.**

As you've seen, there is a fair bit of work to do to turn an idea into a profitable business. Start with understanding yourself and picking ideas that work for you and the world around you. Put some thought and research into your ideas upfront to avoid disappointment later. Set your five safety nets in place. Have a vision and set your values. Create an initial business model and start testing your assumptions step-by-step. Ask your customers questions and pay close attention to what they tell you, verbally and non-verbally. Tweak and refine as you go.

When you have enough information, start rapid experimentation to gather real-time action and data from your customers. Use this data as a feedback loop to iterate and improve as you build and deliver your solution. Position your solution in the market to attract paying customers. Over time, plan how you will convert paying customers into profitable customers.

And boom — just like that, your ideas are out in the world, helping people with their problems and making your business dreams a reality.

If entrepreneurship was easy, everyone would do it. You will have challenges in this process, but the steps in this book simplify the process of becoming an entrepreneur. There will be days you will feel like it's all too much. You will question if it is worth it. On those days, go back to your sweet spot from Chapter One. Remind yourself why this is important for you and the world. Revisit the customer interviews from Chapter Five to remind yourself of challenges that people have shared with you because they have a problem that needs solving. Ask yourself, if not you, then who? If not now, then when?

And remember, I'm always here to listen and talk to you. Challenges along the way stop many people from realising their business dreams. Having a process and a roadmap is great, but it's even better to have someone to speak to as you go through your own individual journey. So, if you feel stuck at any point, reach out to me. I would love to hear from you and help you on your journey.

My mission is to make your transition into entrepreneurship as simple and easy as possible. If you have a dream, I have a way for you to make it a reality. Please contact me at launch@jumpstartstudio.com.au if I can support you through your journey.

My wish is that every person who has ever dreamed of starting a business takes the leap of faith and, with the practical tools and guidance in this book, embarks on a glorious and rewarding adventure.

Make it happen.